The KinderGarden of Eden

How the Modern Liberal Thinks

And Why He's Convinced That Ignorance Is Bliss

EVAN SAYET

DEDICATION

To all the people who asked me not to mention them in this book.

TABLE OF CONTENTS

ACKNOWLEDGMENTS

There are literally scores of people I need to thank for their help in making this book a reality. Fortunately, as noted in the dedication, most don't want me to mention them by name, so that makes this so much easier.

First, I need to thank Brandon Rogers for his talent and dedication. At times Brandon acted as editor, contributed to the cover design, stood up as marketing guru, website designer, sounding board and friend. I could not have gotten this book out on time and have had it turn out as well as it did without him.

Thanks to Vetta Bogdanoff who ably handled the nitty-gritty of editing. Since I was writing and making revisions right up to the last second, this took not just her talents, but also her patience and good cheer. Thank you to Wendy Rae Leaumont for her original work on the cover design.

Thank you, too, to Mary Ann Garner and Kira Newman for their time and good work.

A special thank you to the friends who *will* let me mention them by name, folks who, in many cases, suffered through the most dreadful versions of the book as it came together little by little. These include (in no particular order) Vladimir (Val) Cymbal, Sonja and Mr. Schmidt, Seth Swirsky, Jody Duncan,

Kender MacGowan, Peter Bylsma, Ben Shapiro, Ari David, Fini Goodman, Andrew Klavan, Tony Katz, Kira Davis, John Hawkins, Stacy McCain, Barry Rubin, Larry Greenfield, Ann Marie Murrell, Duane "Bucky" Buckley, Anna and Alex Karpov, Bob and Emilie Golub and Michael Finch.

I'm sure I've left some deserving people out. I apologize and will remedy that in future editions.

And a particular thank you to the folks at the Coffee Bean and Tea Leaf (store # withheld for their safety) for allowing me to turn their facilities into my office, even when they weren't quite sure if I was a dedicated writer burning the midnight oil, or just simply homeless.

A very special thank you to Tom Dreesen, Jon Voight and Gary Sinise for reminding me on a daily basis just exactly what a "mench" is and what I should aspire to be.

And finally, an eternal debt of gratitude to Andrew Breitbart, for being both a friend and a hero. I can think of no better combination.

AUTHOR'S NOTE

The bad news is that you've just spent somewhere around ten dollars to purchase what remains a work in progress. It is the first hundred or so pages of a book I had not planned to publish until sometime in 2013. I'd wanted to hold off until after the elections so that the book would not be seen as so much "political" as philosophical. As more and more of the people I turned to for editorial advice insisted that I get at least this part out before the elections however, I finally relented.

The good news is that, by the time you finish reading these pages, you will understand something that has baffled you for years: how the Modern Liberal thinks and why it is that so many otherwise good, decent, and smart people work on behalf of all that is evil, failed, and wrong and hate— nothing less than hate – anyone who doesn't.

THE LAWS OF MODERN LIBERALISM

1. Indiscriminateness – the total rejection of the intellectual process – is an absolute moral imperative.

2. Indiscriminateness of thought does not lead to indiscriminateness of policies. It leads to siding only and always with the lesser over the better, the wrong over the right, and the evil over the good.

3. Modern Liberal policies occur in tandem. Each effort on behalf of the lesser is met with an equal and opposite campaign against the better.

4. The Modern Liberal will ascribe to the better the negative qualities associated with the lesser while concurrently ascribing to the lesser the positive qualities found in the better.

THE COROLLARIES

1. The Modern Liberal may have personal standards but he must deny them and militate against their use and those who use them in the public arena.

2. The Modern Liberal does not and cannot seek to better himself or society. Instead he must lower others and society to his level.

3. The Modern Liberal has *secondary* policies that are meant only to somewhat mitigate the greater suffering that his primary policies created or exacerbated.

PREFACE

At the Democrats' recent national convention, at least half of the delegates – the most influential activists in the party, each one representing hundreds if not thousands of others in his or her local precinct – voted to eliminate the word "God" from their party's platform. During this same session, these same Democrats voted to undermine the Jews of Israel at the very moment of their greatest peril by no longer recognizing Jerusalem as their capital. The Democrats weren't finished, though. Before the session was out, they had voted to strike the word "rare" from the party's abortion policy.

So what's the Democrats' beef with God? What do they have against the Jews of Israel? Why do they want abortions to be commonplace and frequent? These are just three questions – and they're from just the other day. We Right-Thinking people have a thousand more. And they all come down to this: "Why does the Modern Liberal – the dominant force in today's Democratic Party and throughout so much of America's modern culture – seem to side in every case with evil over good, wrong over right and the behaviors that lead to failure over those that lead to success? This book answers that question.

Before we start, though, it is essential that we define some terms. Most importantly, it must be understood that the "Modern Liberal" is not a liberal who happens to be alive today. Nor is he a Classical Liberal like John F. Kennedy. In fact, he's not liberal at all. The Modern Liberal is as much at war with liberal values as he is with conservative ones. Just consider the difference between Kennedy's admonition to "Ask not what your country can do for you – ask what you can do for your country," and the Modern Liberal's belief that your country should do virtually everything for you (see Barack Obama's "Julia"). Meanwhile, the Modern Liberal finds the notion of doing things for their country repugnant as, being "Citizens of The World," such provincialism is seen by them as nothing short of "xenophobic."

Modern Liberalism is an entirely separate ideology, new in its prevalence – and now dominance – to what I call the Modern Liberal era (post World War II through today). In fact, I call it Modern *Liberalism* only because *they* typically call themselves Liberals and I felt that any other word would make their prevalence and power appear less than it is. I added the modifier "Modern" to make clear that they are not what they say they are, nor what the Liberals used to be.

It is also essential to understand that, while Modern Liberalism is fully in control of today's Democratic Party, not everyone who votes Democrat is a Modern Liberal. Many – like some union members, government workers and welfare recipients for example – may vote Democrat for practical and self-serving reasons rather than ideological ones.

Finally, while I tend to speak in absolutes – as one does when describing adherents to an ideology ("The Marxist believes this," or the "Buddhist does that") – people are people and thus a mass of contradictions. They are in possession of limited information, personality quirks and other flesh-and-blood realities that make an individual an individual. Nonetheless, the traits of the Modern Liberal discussed throughout appear so consistently in those I describe as to make my statements true...and the Modern Liberal dangerous.

****

I first began to investigate how the Modern Liberal thinks in the wake of the September 11th terrorist attacks. In fact, I call myself a "9-13 Republican."

I do so not because it took me two extra days to understand the significance of the massacres but because, frankly, they didn't surprise me. Of course I didn't know the date and I didn't know the targets, but even as a New York City-born, (then) Liberal Jew, I knew just enough about the realities of the world to know that the same people who were massacring the Jews of Israel and people of other religions and cultures in places all around the globe because they were the *closest* infidels, would, when they could, come to murder the *biggest* infidels – the so called "Great Satan."

What surprised me is what I call "9-12." That's my shorthand for the days, weeks, months and now years *after* 9-11 and my fellow Liberals' response to the attacks. The idea that we *deserved* it – that it was, in the words of Barack Obama's "spiritual mentor," Jeremiah Wright, "The chickens coming home to roost" – and that the way to prevent further attacks was to be *nicer* to the terrorists was insane to me.

Here we were facing the most obvious case of good versus evil of my lifetime and those I'd thought were the good and smart guys – the Liberals – were not only taking the side of evil, but they were often making the most objectively false and even hateful anti-American arguments in order to do so.

Why was this? How could this be? This is what I needed to know, and it is what I began to study, contemplate, discuss and debate for what has now been more than a decade.

About five years ago, I presented my thesis on "How the Modern Liberal Thinks" in a lecture to the Heritage Foundation in Washington, D.C. I began the talk by saying, "I've got to imagine that just about every one of us in this room recognizes that the Democrats are wrong on just about every issue. Well, I'm here to propose to you that it's not just 'just about' every issue; it's quite literally every issue. And it's not just wrong; it's as wrong as wrong can be."

Half a decade later, I am even more convinced that the Modern Liberal is, in fact, as wrong as wrong can be on quite literally every issue. That is, I have no doubt that he will at every turn side with the lesser over the better, the wrong over the right, the ugly over the beautiful, the vulgar over the refined, the behaviors that lead to failure over those that lead to success and, first and foremost, with the evil over the good.

The question, then, becomes: "why?" Why do so many seemingly nice, caring, and in every other way smart people make the most ludicrous and hateful arguments on behalf of all that is evil, failed and wrong? Why is so much of their enmity aimed at all that is good, right and successful?

And the explanation I offered over the next forty or so minutes in 2007 was so satisfying to so many that this little wonkish talk by this then-unknown political commentator went viral on the Internet. Andrew Breitbart called that talk "one of the five most important conservative speeches ever given." It has even been used by one of the nation's leading intelligence experts to create a computer program to help anticipate terrorist attacks from Leftist groups like the New Black Panthers and Leftist enemies like Hugo Chavez.

But as the talk was beginning to go viral, I was reminded that a scientific theory – even in the softest of soft sciences like psychology, sociology and political science – is not recognized as true simply because it offers an elegant, powerful and satisfying explanation of events that have already taken place. In order for a theory to be accepted as true, one has to be able to use it to be able to anticipate and predict behaviors that have not yet come to be.

Clearly, back in 2007, there was no way I could have known that Barack Obama would be the Democratic Party's nominee, or that by the end of the following year he'd be elected president of the United States – much less that, as president, he would bow down before some world leaders but not others. Yet, my theory anticipated to perfection that *if* a President Obama *did* bow down before some world leaders but not others, it would be to the despotic king of Saudi Arabia (the home of 15 of the 19 terrorists who massacred thousands of Americans on 9-11) and to the symbol of the Japanese imperialism that brought us the attack on Pearl Harbor and the Bataan Death March to whom he would bow but *not* to the Queen of England.

And, while back in 2007, I couldn't possibly have known just who would and wouldn't give a future President Obama gifts, my theory had anticipated to perfection that a Modern Liberal president would gladly accept an anti-America propaganda book from the socialist dictator, Hugo Chavez, while unceremoniously returning the gift of a bust of Winston Churchill to our friends in Great Britain.

And I couldn't have known that someday a *President* Obama would order NASA to use its dwindling resources to honor one religion, while at the same time spitting in the face of the leaders of two others. Still, my theory anticipated *to perfection* that *if* a Modern Liberal president *were* to do these things, it would be Islam that he would seek to honor while it would be the Jew, Benjamin Netanyahu, he would publicly shun at the very moment of Israel's greatest peril and the peace-loving Dalai Lama, he would force to exit the White House past the Obama family's trash.

And while, of course, there was no way that I could have known in 2007 just where revolutions would crop up across the globe during a future Obama administration; my theory anticipated to perfection that *if* they popped up where they eventually did, a Modern Liberal president would oppose the democratic uprising in Iran, support the overthrow of America's friend Hosni Mubarak in Egypt, call for a coup to replace an allied democracy in Honduras, "lead from behind" in Libya and do nothing while a second-generation mass murderer mowed his own people down in the streets in Syria.

My theory was able to anticipate every one of these actions because I knew that the Modern Liberal – whether it was Barack Obama or anyone else who shared his ideology – would follow the Four Laws of the Unified Field Theory of Liberalism and its Corollaries. And because they would I knew that the Modern Liberal would in every case side with the lesser over the better, the wrong over the right and the evil over the good.

CHAPTER I

THE IDEOLOGUES AND THE BRAIN DEAD

"Objectivity is impossible, and it is also undesirable.
That is, if it were possible it would be undesirable."
– Howard Zinn

First it must be understood that there are, in fact, *two* kinds of Modern Liberals – the True Believer and his Mindless Foot Soldier. This is easy to miss since there is absolutely no difference between the two when it comes to the policies they support or oppose or in the rhetoric they employ in their efforts. They both follow the laws and the corollaries of the Unified Field Theory in every way, and they each end up working, only and always, on behalf of all that is evil, failed, and wrong and against all that is good, right, and successful. In fact, this may seem like a distinction without a difference. But it's a distinction nonetheless – one that is essential in understanding how the Modern Liberal thinks.

What differentiates the True Believer from his Mindless Foot Soldier is found in Howard Zinn's quotation at the top of the page.

Keep in mind that Zinn was not some little-known oddball that I plucked out of obscurity to help me make my point. He was arguably the most beloved and influential Modern Liberal of all, a man who counts amongst his accomplishments that he is the author of the single most assigned text on America and American history in the country's primary schools and colleges.

The Mindless Foot Soldier subscribes to the first part of Zinn's claim. He has for all intents and purposes been brainwashed – most significantly by the "education" system he first entered at the age of five and didn't leave for almost two decades (and sometimes longer) – to believe that objectivity is impossible.

Since he believes that objectivity is impossible, the Mindless Foot Soldier does not and will not engage his intellect to seek out the rightful answers. Whatever he might discover through the process, he's convinced, would be at best merely his own "point-of-view" – a point of view that, by definition, would be no more right and no more valid than any and every other.

Since he believes all points of view are equally right and equally valid, the Mindless Foot Soldier is convinced that anyone who would declare his own point of view right or another point of view wrong is and can only be a bigot (for his side) or a phobic (against the other).

The True Believer, on the other hand, subscribes to the *second* part of Zinn's statement. He rejects the use of his intellect not because he thinks objectivity is impossible, but because he knows that its product – the truth – is *undesirable*.

This is because the True Believer is an ideologue with a utopian vision, and, as with both ideologues and those with utopian visions, the truth invariably gets in the way.

Here an essential distinction must be drawn between intellect and what I'll call "intellectualism." For my purposes throughout the book, the former is the use of one's mind to discover the rightful answers. The latter, on the other hand, is the use of one's mind only to conjure clever explanations for what is already believed. Seeing objectivity as impossible or undesirable, the Modern Liberal wholly rejects the intellect and engages only in intellectualism – something many people then confuse for "smarts."

Although he wouldn't conceive of it in this manner, the True Believer's utopian vision is predicated on the notion that if mankind lost paradise when Adam and Eve ate the apple and gained the knowledge of good and evil (and its little sisters - right and wrong, better and worse, and so on) then mankind can return to paradise if only everyone would just "regurgitate the apple" and give up all recognition of the existence of the better.

To the True Believer, then, indiscriminateness – the total rejection of the intellectual process – is a moral imperative because it holds the key to returning to paradise.

For the True Believer to come to this conclusion he must be convinced of something for which there is no logic or evidence and which stands in utter opposition to everything else he believes (or says he believes) about God and man. He must be convinced that the human being is born morally perfect and is only then corrupted by evil forces within society seeking to use him to advance their own self-serving agendas. He must believe, as the philosopher Jean-Jacques Rousseau said, "Everything is good as it leaves the hands of the Author of things; everything degenerates in the hands of man."

Just who turned the first morally perfect human being "evil" is never quite explained – nor is how the existence of an "Author" who creates morally perfect beings jibes with the Modern Liberal's usual antipathy for God and religion. The Mindless Foot Soldier, however, needs no explanation, for he wouldn't use his mind to ponder it, and the True Believer is happy to not have to provide one.

If the Modern Liberal is right – if the human being is born morally perfect – then the True Believer's Utopia is not only possible, it is easily achieved. All the True Believer would need to do is find some way to retard the child's moral and intellectual growth at a level prior to his being corrupted by society and a morally perfect world would result.

To accomplish this goal, the True Believer needs a mechanism for preventing children from learning and adults from believing their eyes. That mechanism is to make a moral imperative out of the rejection of objective facts, objective standards and objective logic – to declare objectivity itself "impossible" on the one hand and "undesirable" on the other.

HOW IT BEGAN

Prior to the Modern Liberal era, the unrivaled success of Western Civilization was due to the healthy balance that was struck between the scientific and the extra-scientific, between craft and art, between the tangible and the imagination or, in my favorite locution, between Athens and Jerusalem.

This balance was not as the Leftists portray it today, wherein science and the extra-scientific are mutually exclusive and wholly at odds with one another. Rather, there was the recognition that both the scientific and the extra-scientific – both the cold, hard facts and the warmer, human things like love, morality, decency, beauty, justice, and mercy – were necessary for creating and maintaining a well functioning, happy, healthy, prosperous and progressing society.

In fact, in the Vatican – the supposed ground zero for religion's war against science – there are, and have long been, two spectacular murals of equal size and equal grandeur taking up the whole of opposing walls. On one side are the great people and great moments from religious history, and on the other are the great people and great moments from science. Far from Western religions ever being at war with science, they actually took great pride in how, time and again, science seemed to prove God's majesty.

While in the old world religion tended to hold the upper hand – and was sometimes (though not nearly as often as it is currently portrayed) even antagonistic to some of the latest scientific finds – this was more a matter of practicality than superstition or oppression.

It was simply a matter of survival that, back before modern technologies allowed those who had erred to extricate themselves from dangerous situations with just a phone call to 911 or the taking of a pill to cure whatever it was that then suddenly ailed them, society needed people to be better able to police and take care of themselves. This they were encouraged to do through stricter moral teachings and the reminder that they were being watched by a just and moral God who expected the same of them.

Then along came the "Enlightenment," the peaceful dawning of which dispels the notion that science and religion were (or are) enemies. The Enlightenment, however, didn't seek to merely readjust the balance between Athens and Jerusalem – it sought to wholly eliminate God from the equation.

The Enlightenment was all about "pure science." If something couldn't be measured, quantified, or recreated in the laboratory, then it simply wasn't true. Since things like love, beauty, morality, decency, justice and mercy can't be measured or recreated in a lab, they were soon eliminated from the "enlightened" world. The death of the extra-scientific was famously proclaimed with Nietzsche's announcement that "God is dead."

The Enlightenment surely brought some great advances, but as science more and more replaced the extra-scientific, some – most famously Rousseau – noticed the high price.

The pushback went 180-degrees. As historian Allan Bloom explains, "Here Rousseau bursts on the scene, just at the moment of Enlightenment's victory," condemning cold science for seeking progress that was devoid of the human traits of "community, virtue, compassion, feeling, enthusiasm, the beautiful and the sublime..."

Rather than seeking to readjust the balance – to reintroduce God to science – Rousseau sought a total reversal, the complete replacement of science with nothing but the innate passions. Describing him as "an inverse Socrates," Bloom concluded that "reason itself" was rejected by Rousseau's new philosophy.

Whereas science without the extra-scientific could not produce anything but a cold, heartless machine, passion without intellect could not raise the individual above the level of the infant. In fact, one of Rousseau's more famous contemporaries, Voltaire, wrote to the philosopher:

> *I have received your new book against the human race, and thank you for it. Never was such a cleverness used in the design of making us all stupid. One longs, in reading your book, to walk on all fours. But as I have lost that habit for more than sixty years, I feel unhappily the impossibility of resuming it.*

Rousseau's ideas found a few followers – mostly amongst the leisure class and those who bandied about words for a living (which then, as now, tended to be one and the same) – but, for the next two hundred years or so, Voltaire's take was the general consensus and the Enlightenment rushed on.

Only when the Enlightenment reached its inevitable soulless extremes – when Darwin's scientific theory of "the survival of the fittest," untamed by the extra-scientific qualities of morality, empathy, mercy, decency and justice manifested itself in the Holocaust – did the Enlightenment disqualify itself as the philosophy that might finally bring peace and universal prosperity. To the contrary, the Holocaust suggested to many that reason is the most monstrous of all of man's faculties.

The logic of this conclusion was faulty, of course, as it was not science that had led to the Holocaust, but rather science untamed by the extra-scientific – science without God – that had. But as the shaken world looked to rise from the literal ashes of the Enlightenment, the earliest Modern Liberals didn't seek to resurrect God as a means of taming pure science. Instead, they left the "dead" God in his grave – and threw science in on top of him.

In the Modern Liberal era, Athens and Jerusalem lay in ruins. It is a time with neither God nor science. It is a time with neither truth nor beauty. In the Modern Liberal era, it is indiscriminateness – the total rejection of the intellect – that reigns as not just "a" but "the" moral imperative of the age.

Not surprisingly then, in this era, "greatness" would have no relationship to God or science or their off-shoots like art and craft.

In fact, exactly the opposite would be true. In the Modern Liberal era, then, a photograph of a cross floating in a man's urine would become the stuff of award-winning "art", vulgar ditties like the song "Fuck You" would be deemed by the supposed experts one of the "best" compositions of the year and musings emanating from a sex organ – the *Vagina Monologues* – would be seen as "great" theater.

Science, too, fell victim to this new ideology. The scientific "truth" would now no longer be what was found though fact, evidence and reason but would be determined only and always by the needs of this new Cult of Indiscriminateness. AIDS, for example, would be declared an "equal opportunity disease" not because it was, but because the indiscriminate needed it to be to ensure it would receive the research funds and attention the Modern Liberal felt it deserved, and, just as importantly, to ensure that homosexuality wasn't seen as in any way "different" or "bad."

In fact, since indiscriminateness had become nothing less than a moral imperative, anyone who would attempt to use God and science to question the vulgar, infantile, and ultimately failed products of Modern Liberalism was seen as not just "wrong" in his conclusions, but *evil* in his heart – or, in Thomas Sowell's phrase, he was deemed "Not merely in error but in sin."

Dennis Prager notes that "Republicans think the Democrat is stupid; Democrats think the Republican is evil." This is because, to Right-Thinking people, those who reject discriminating thought *are* stupid. In fact, they are as stupid as the five-year-old child who does not yet have the intellectual wherewithal to be a discriminating thinker. To the Modern Liberal, those who engage in discriminating thought are evil because they discriminate.

So disdainful of intellect was the Modern Liberal in fact, that one of them would proudly declare – and millions more would signal their agreement with their wallets and turn his book into one of the biggest literary phenomena of all time – that *All I Really Need To Know I Learned in Kindergarten*.

PROGRESSIVE REGRESSION

That they themselves would dub this ideology "Progressive" is just another example of how every one of the Modern Liberals' beliefs (or stated beliefs) is not merely wrong but as wrong as wrong can be. Not only could a world without God or science not progress, but the entire purpose of Modern Liberalism was to so totally regress humanity that mankind would return to the very first days of man on earth.

In this Utopia that the True Believer envisions, everyone would be like Adam and Eve in the Garden of Eden, or, more precisely the secular version - the five-year-old child in another sort of garden paradise: the kindergarten. According to the True Believer's Blueprint for Utopia, everyone was to live in total ignorance and therefore (or so the promise went) in total bliss.

THE PURPOSE OF PURPOSELESSNESS

Since the True Believer's goal is the total regression of man back to his first days on earth, it wasn't enough for the Modern Liberal to simply ignore God and science, he had to become their enemies. He had to seek a world not only without them, but a world in opposition to them. In order to return man to Eden, the Modern Liberal had to reverse all of mankind's progress, attacking everything that history had accomplished and undoing all that Athens and Jerusalem – reason and faith – had ever or would ever create. Note Voltaire's recognition that Rousseau's efforts were *"against* the human race," and the results were to have everyone again "walk on all fours."

To reverse the course of humanity, the True Believers had to turn everything on its head, literally changing the very meaning of life and the purpose of man's day-to-day existence. Whereas Western Civilization was predicated on a person using his allotted days to *better* himself, without God or science the Modern Liberal had neither the mandate nor the means to do so. In fact, the Modern Liberal was taught from his birth to *never* seek to better himself in any way. This was because the Modern Liberal knew that to discover the better would require people to use that most monstrous of their faculties – their mind. Instead, in the Modern Liberal era, the child was instructed to only and always just *be* himself. The same "self" he had been from the day he was born.

Similarly, in the past, good people spent their lives trying to do good things and society encouraged them to do so. But, without God or science, the Modern Liberal again had neither the mandate nor the means to pursue the good. In fact, he was taught from his birth to *never* attempt to do good things, for, the Modern Liberal knew, that for him to recognize the good would require him to employ his potentially corrupted mind. Rather than seek to *do* good, he was instructed to do only and always what *feels* good.

In fact, "if it feels good, do it" was one of the founding mantras of the cult, with the True Believer convinced that if the child were led by his pure feelings and not his tainted mind he would then be led to *do* good.

And, according to the True Believer, the child would continue to do the good and right things throughout the whole of his life, but only so long as he remained uncorrupted by society and its evil and self-serving lessons. The True Believer was convinced that paradise would be regained, but only so long as the Modern Liberal remained morally and intellectually retarded at the level of the small child.

Meanwhile, the Modern Liberal child – having been convinced (mostly via the schools but through other channels as well) of his own moral perfection and that he was in possession of a point of view as valid as any and all who had ever lived – would remain permanently retarded for he would have nothing he needed to learn and no one he respected enough to learn from. He would be convinced that all he ever needed to know he'd learned by the time he'd finished kindergarten.

In fact, at this time, the very purpose of learning was spun on its head. In the Modern Liberal era, people didn't seek to acquire knowledge for the purpose of becoming smarter and better. Instead everyone started out perfect and then spent their lives "learning to love themselves" as they were, which – as one of the Modern Liberal era's keenest cultural observers, Dr. Jean M. Twenge reminds us in *Generation Me* – was deemed both in song and in practice "The Greatest Love of All."

The retardation that comes from self-adoration was the very centerpiece of the True Believers' Blueprint for Utopia, and for this reason they made self-love paramount and reinforced it on a near-constant basis through incessant programs of wholly unmerited "self-esteem"-building. You were perfect just for being you, which meant that the only way not to be perfect (and perhaps even turn into one of those evil bigots and phobics) was to attempt to change (i.e. better) yourself in any way.

"Be yourself," "do what feels good" and "esteem nothing more than yourself" were the new pillars of society in the Modern Liberal era, and they were in every way the exact opposite of what had made

Western Civilization great and the very antithesis of what was needed for a functioning, happy, healthy, prosperous and progressing society.

In fact, not only were these concepts not progressive, but they couldn't possibly have been more *regressive* (just as the True Believers wished) as they made "feelings" – the same "feelings" that every child since the dawn of man was born with – into the arbiter of all truths; while they eliminated that which does progress with time – personal and collective wisdom.

A POINTLESS POINT OF VIEW

Since the Unified Field Theory of Liberalism states that all Modern Liberal policies occur in tandem, the True Believers' efforts to elevate the naive and inexperienced child (the lesser) in esteem, stature, power and reward were met with an equal and opposite effort to denigrate and weaken the better – the knowledgeable and experienced adult. Thus, whereas Western Civilization taught their children to "respect their elders" and "honor their mothers and fathers," the child in the Modern Liberal era was instructed "don't trust anyone over thirty" and "question authority."

It was not a coincidence that the True Believers chose thirty as the age when someone would suddenly – almost magically – go from trustworthy to untrustworthy. In the Modern Liberal era, thirty would become the age when the child might finally first grow up and reject the shackles of retardation that Modern Liberalism requires. It was exactly the age when an adult might return and tell the children that they'd tested the theories taught in the Modern Liberal classrooms against the real world and found them not only deeply wanting, but profoundly dangerous and destructive.

In fact, as Diane West reminds us in *The Death of the Grown-Up*, it was during the Modern Liberal era that the National Academy of Sciences actually changed the official definition of "adolescence" so that childhood wouldn't end until the age of thirty.

Meanwhile, it is simply a truism that when children get to "question authority" it is they who become the authority. This, then, is how a pre-school in my neighborhood tries to convince parents in the Modern Liberal era to send their children to their academy:

> *At our school, teachers and children learn together...*
> *Let your child be a partner in their education...*
> *At HDC Your Child Leads The Way.*

But, of course, with little knowledge or experience, the child doesn't possess the tools needed to rightly judge just who is and isn't truly authoritative in their fields. This leaves the child with only his "feelings" to determine who he'll respect and agree to learn from.

Since the truth of the real world is sometimes sad – and never utopian – those who spoke the truth hurt the children's feelings and thus were then (and forevermore) rejected. Only those who reinforced the infantile beliefs of the children were embraced by them as being truly in the know.

In fact, those who spoke the truth were not only rejected, they were reviled. After all, the authoritative are, by definition, recognized by society to have a better point of view than others. That's something that the Mindless Foot Soldier is sure can only be the result of society's bigotries and phobias and that the True Believer, in the service of his Blueprint for Utopia, simply declares to be so.

In fact, those who spoke the truth were considered doubly evil, for the immutable laws of God and science they spoke of were, in Sowell's word, "constraints" that prevented the child from accomplishing the three pillars of his ideology: be yourself, do only what feels good, and hold yourself in higher esteem than any and all others.

In the real world, the child can't continue to forever just be himself if he expects to survive. He must better himself. He can't just do whatever feels good and expect to enjoy peace-of-mind and good relationships in this life and the potential for salvation in the next. He must do good.

Most devastatingly, if the Modern Liberal were to acknowledge the existence of the truly authoritative, he'd have to admit that the better does exist. This would destroy the entire predicate of the True Believer's utopian ideology and force the Mindless Foot Soldier to admit that, morally and intellectually retarded at the level of the small child, it isn't him.

To the Modern Liberal, ignorance is the most cherished of all traits. It is, in fact, nothing less than the single moral imperative by which he lives his life. His "intellectualism" – the sometimes clever verbiage he uses to cover for his naiveté and ignorance – should not be confused with intelligence.

To the Mindless Foot Soldier, the rejection of rational thought and elevated standards – God and science – is a moral imperative because he sees it as the means to finally eliminate all of the world's bigotries and phobias and the "social injustices" that they cause.

To the True Believer, ignorance is the most cherished of all things because it is the means for man to, once and for all, return to Paradise.

Thought of in reverse, the True Believer knows that it was the acquisition of knowledge that ended Adam and Eve's time in Eden. And it is the acquisition of knowledge that ends the five-year-old's blissful years of carefree existence. This has convinced the True Believer that the great evil of the world – the only thing keeping man from returning to paradise – is the adult's acquired knowledge of right and wrong, good and evil, better and worse, beautiful and ugly and all of the other things that then require the grown-up to engage in discriminating thought in his pursuit of the better.

FOREVER (VERY) YOUNG

When I say the Modern Liberal is morally and intellectually retarded at the level of the five-year-old child, it is not hyperbole; it's a diagnosis. And it's a diagnosis that, as we shall see, is shared by a good many others – including, albeit typically unwittingly, many Modern Liberals themselves. For now, here's how Dr. Dan Kiley put it in his 1983 *New York Times* bestseller, *The Peter Pan Syndrome*:

> *Look to your children, or to the child of a friend. And ask yourself: what would happen if his body grew up but his mind didn't?*

The reason that this retardation occurs at the age of five and not say, three, seven or ten, is that five is exactly the age at which something happens to virtually every American child: he enters kindergarten. It is then and there that the Modern Liberal "educators" (the same educators who adore an historian, Zinn, who declares objectivity "undesirable") get control of America's children on a full-time basis for the first time. And it is from that moment and for the next several decades – the whole of his formative years and then some – that the child is taught the pillars of the Cult of Indiscriminateness and where he is then rewarded and punished on no other basis than his adherence to the rules of the cult.

That it is, in fact, on no other basis that the child is then rewarded and punished is proved by the simple fact that, today in America, a child is far more likely to graduate from high school (and even college) illiterate and incapable of basic calculation than he is to not believe objectivity is impossible.

The effects of the Modern Liberal's retardation go further than just his policies and rhetoric. Almost from the start of the Modern Liberal era, psychologists and sociologists, pollsters and keen cultural observers have noticed new pathologies and social trends afflicting the Modern Liberal individually and Modern Liberal society as a whole. These are things I discuss in greater detail in the full version of the book due out in mid-2013.

While many have offered ad hoc explanations for these new conditions – the rise and spread of the mental illness of adult (or permanent) narcissism (which experts such as Drs. Twenge and W. Keith Campbell recognize to now be "epidemic"), the destruction of the social fabric detailed by Harvard Professor Robert Putnam, an unhappiness that bleeds over into clinical depression and more – only the Unified Field Theory of Liberalism and the retardation of the Modern Liberal explains them all and explains them all easily.

Finally, keep in mind as you read that the fact that the Modern Liberal is morally and intellectually retarded at the level of the five-year-old child does not mean that he isn't marvelously clever. It means only, as Voltaire wrote, it's a "cleverness used in the design of making us all stupid." It doesn't mean that Modern Liberals can't be terrifically articulate, only that, as Sowell observed, their "articulateness" is nothing more than a certain "verbal nimbleness (that) allows them to elude all fact and reason."

Their words are what Dwight Eisenhower called "exquisite nonsense," and if they weren't so dangerous and destructive, one could smile and pat the Modern Liberal on the head and tell him how cute he is and go on about the business of being an adult.

But he is dangerous and destructive, with the True Believer's very purpose being the total destruction of everything that God and science – most imperatively Western Civilization – has ever created. This effort is even more dangerous because, having been brainwashed from the youngest of ages, the True Believer's Mindless Foot Soldiers just mindlessly go along in support. And, for this reason – the further explanation of which is the primary purpose of this book – the Modern Liberal will invariably and, in fact, inevitably side with evil over good, wrong over right and the behaviors that lead to failure over those that lead to success.

I WILL SURVIVE

Of course, if I'm right – if the Modern Liberal is, in fact, both morally and intellectually retarded at the level of the five-year-old child – I'll need to explain how it is that he manages to survive (and sometimes even appears to thrive) in the real world. The answer to that question is the other major purpose of this book, and I begin to provide it in the next chapter.

For now, suffice it to say that stupidity is a luxury. One can only afford to be naive and ignorant so long as he lives in a world of great plenty. Adam and Eve could only survive their ignorance and naiveté because God provided such abundance. When God no longer provided that bounty, they had to either grow up or die. The kindergartner can only survive such ignorance and naiveté because there are parents who provide for his every need. When the parents no longer do so, the child must either grow up or die. It's not at all surprising, then, that an ideology whose very purpose is to retard the individuals' moral and intellectual growth at the level of the small child would, after centuries of being rejected, suddenly find a home in the most luxurious time and the most luxurious place in all of human history – America after the Second World War.

CHAPTER II

AN OVERVIEW FROM THE BOTTOM

Like Adam and Eve just prior to eating from the apple, the Modern Liberal has never had a mature thought in his life. That is, he has never once attempted to gather the facts, study the evidence and weigh these things in a rational formulation in order to seek out the rightful answers. This is because, like Adam and Eve in Eden, he's never once had to.

The Modern Liberal was born into a life as close to paradise as any human being since God first created man. Having come of age in or after the 1960s, virtually everything that virtually every other human being, in literally every other time and in literally every other place, had had to think about – at its most basic, how to avoid things like disease, hunger, poverty and physical pain – had all but been eradicated just prior to the Modern Liberal's entry into the sentient world.

It's easy to forget – or just to have never thought about it at all – but America after the Second World War was not only unlike anything man had ever known, it was, in fact, the culmination of a "five-thousand year leap" forward in time. It was *eons* ahead of the technologies and medicines from not just earlier millennia or earlier centuries but, in many important ways, from just years and even months before. And every new dawn brought the promise – if not yet the achievement – of still another miraculous stride.

Thanks to the recent advances of Western Civilization in general and the Great Generations of Americans in particular (where the near-perfect balance between God and science had been struck), things like polio, chicken pox, smallpox, the flu as a death sentence and virtually any and every other monstrous disease that had plagued humanity – including the plague – were simply never part of the Modern Liberal's life and therefore played no part in the Modern Liberal's "thinking."

From the time of his birth, poverty was so near to extinction that just to be able to call any American save for the utter fringe (most notably the drug-addled and the mentally ill) "impoverished" required that an entirely new definition be invented – a definition of such fabulous riches that it is easily conceivable that even kings and tsars and popes of yore might well have happily traded for it. Such, in fact, was the plot of the Eddie Murphy/Arsenio Hall movie *Coming to America*. And that was a *modern-day* kingdom.

During this time hunger became so easily avoidable that anyone who found a dollar in the street could enjoy a three-course gourmet meal prepared by a world-class chef, available for effortless microwaving at any of tens of thousands of *99 Cents Only* and *Dollar Stores*. In fact, those born into this time and this place need never have even long suffered a headache or a charley horse as a drug recognized as nothing less than a miracle by those who had lived without it - aspirin – was never not in their lives and never not just a few steps away.

From the dawn of time until the dawn of the Modern Liberal era people had had to think – they had had to use their intellect in order to discover and then practice the better ways – because being wrong came with the potential for dire consequences. For millions and millions born in America after the Second World War, with these potential consequences all but eliminated, thinking became a relic, their mind nearly as unneeded and unused as their appendix.

HO-HEIGH, HO-HEIGH, IT'S HOME FROM WORK STAY I

With disease, hunger, poverty and physical pain nearly all but vanquished, there was only one other consequence of man's having "eaten the apple" that made the Modern Liberal's day-to-day life anything less than utopian: the need to toil for his reward. By the time the Modern Liberal came of age, technology had nearly eradicated this last scourge as well.

From the dawn of time until just before the Modern Liberal was born, people had had to hunt, fish or farm. They had had to make and mend their clothing. They had had to know how to groom, tend and ride a horse, raise livestock, chop wood, stoke fires, cook and preserve their food and do a thousand other chores as simply a matter of course and a requisite for survival. These people had had to be smart (i.e. right) because being stupid led to things that the Modern Liberal has likely never seen and knows next to nothing about: things like real deprivation, debilitating injuries and premature death.

By the time the Modern Liberal came of age, almost none of these efforts were necessary and, save for on a lark or as a hobby, only a very few would ever do any (much less all) of them. Even when they did, technology had made these things so free of effort – and in turn, need for intellect – that they barely resembled the practices that continued to bear their names. Simply compare what cooking dinner or getting water, washing your clothes or just staying warm – if you even could stay warm – required in any other time and in any other place from the dawn of man until just before the Modern Liberal's birth.

Of course, even in the Modern Liberal era, *some* people had to do things. *Somebody* had to make all those microwavable dinners and the disposable dishes in which they would come, and *somebody* had to invent and produce first the high-speed vacuum cleaner, then the self-propelled vacuum cleaner and now the robotic vacuum cleaner that requires of the Modern Liberal not even so much as a nudge. And, yes, of course, *some* people had to continue to farm the land, raise the cattle, and milk the cows so that everyone else could eat cheaply and eat well. But as technology built upon technology fewer and fewer Americans were required to do much of anything at all. And, when you don't do anything, you really can just "be yourself" and do whatever "feels good" because, when you don't do anything, nothing can go wrong.

WHAT TO DO WHEN THERE'S NOTHING TO DO

Both because there was nothing much to do and because with nothing much to do they'd never learned to do very much, the more clever Modern Liberals flocked to industries where neither toil nor intelligence was required. These were the "Rhetoric Industries" where verbal nimbleness and not actual accomplishment was the coin of the realm. They were lucrative – often extremely lucrative – fields where oratorical and literary canniness and not tangible results proved the "rightness" of one's claim and the "intelligence" of its claimant.

These clever Modern Liberals became academics and journalists, entertainers and psychologists, politicians and community organizers, "rights activists" and social workers, and other such things where words were the entirety of both their product and their effort.

Entering these fields did not *preclude* intelligence, it simply made it unnecessary. And, as the Modern Liberals more and more took over these fields, each successive generation would be even further entrenched in the ideology of indiscriminateness for those in power would hire, promote and in other ways reward only those who firmly adhered to the dictates of The Cult.

For the clever folks in the Rhetoric Industries, there was no reason to use their intellect to seek out the better ways of doing things since, since they didn't do anything, there were no better ways of doing them. There was no reason for them to use their intellect to seek out the better ways of making things since, since they didn't make anything, there were no better ways of making them. Since they didn't do or make anything, there was no incentive for them to do it or make it right. And since they didn't do or make anything, there were no consequences for them in doing it or making it wrong. Most importantly, since they didn't do anything or make anything, there were no lessons to be learned from their experiences.

Having gone from the paradise of childhood to the utopia of the Rhetoric Industries (the word "utopia," in fact, means "A place made of words"), all these folks would ever do is talk. And when you don't do anything, you don't even need to know what you're talking about because, when you don't do anything, nothing can go wrong.

GEE, THIS EVIL TASTES SO GOOD

In paradise there is no need to think deeply about extra-scientific things like justice, mercy and beauty, for, in paradise, justice is a given, mercy is unneeded, and by definition, ugliness doesn't exist. This is why, for example, to the Modern Liberal, even that photograph of the crucifix in urine is "beautiful" (and anyone who say it's not is not just wrong but evil.)

And, in paradise, there's no need to ponder the scientific, for what better outcome could investigation or experimentation bring than paradise itself? Even if one were disposed to contemplation about things like God and science, how would he test his theories when the results are not only always the same but always utopian?

In such a world, rhetoric – clever verbiage without weight or consequence – reigns as king. In fact, it is the be-all and end-all of one's efforts. So obvious is this fact that the very name of the crown jewel of the Rhetoric Industries, Academia, has become a well-known synonym for "clever verbiage without weight or consequence," as in, "Eh, it's all academic anyway; let's go *do* something."

The entire "job" of those in the Rhetoric Industries, then, is to take one of the Modern Liberal's infantile beliefs and invent the oratorical or literary razzle-dazzle necessary to give it a "sophisticated" and "grown-up" sound. The entire purpose is to reject the intellect in favor of "intellectualism." In fact, this is exactly what Robert Fulghum, the author of *All I Really Need to Know I Learned in Kindergarten*, advises his millions of devoted followers:

> *Take any one of those items [the lessons taught in the kindergarten classroom] and extrapolate it into sophisticated adult terms and apply it to your family life or your work or your government or your world and it holds true and clear and firm.*

In other words, even by their own account, the *terminology* that the Modern Liberal employs may become more "sophisticated"-sounding with time, and the size of the words he uses to intellectualize may become more "adult-like" through the years, but the infantile concepts upon which the Modern Liberal bases his policies remain unchanged from the time he's an infant to the time he passes on. This is not just my opinion – it's Fulghum and his millions of fans', too.

Ernest Hemingway recognized that "the shortest [way to an] answer" is to stop talking and start "doing the thing." Those in the Rhetoric Industries would never stop talking and never start doing anything, because, living in paradise where there are no questions, the Modern Liberal doesn't need answers.

Without right or wrong everything becomes just a matter of taste and the alternatives merely different flavors. To the Modern Liberal, then, any attempt to use God or science to argue on behalf of one "flavor" over another – say Western civilization over Islam –

would be like trying to make a moral or scientific argument on behalf of chocolate over strawberry ice cream.

Those who would seek moral or scientific proof of a "flavor's" superiority, then, could be nothing more than fools, while those who would claim to have found such proof could be nothing other than bigots or phobics – or perhaps just evil and greedy liars with stock in the chocolate company.

Stupid, bigoted, phobic, evil and greedy are, of course, the *only* explanations that the Modern Liberal can or does offer to explain why Right-Thinking people don't join him in support of his latest godless, anti-scientific, utterly infantile, and invariably failed schemes. In fact, take a second and try to think of a single argument that the Modern Liberal offers regarding *any* issue that doesn't consist in its entirety of "we're right because (our grandiose self-esteem tells us) we're morally and intellectually superior, and anyone who disagrees with us is (1) stupid, (2) bigoted, (3) phobic, (4) greedy or (5) evil." The truth is you can't name one. Not one. Seriously, try it.

There is simply no way to disagree with the Modern Liberal *even in the slightest* on *any* issue and not fall into one of these categories. This is why it really *doesn't* matter what your "sign" says, they'll still say it's "racist."

This is because, to the Modern Liberal, anything other than indiscriminateness proves that discrimination has taken place. You might be discriminating because you're stupid or because you're evil or because there's money to be made in it, but, no matter what, by engaging in discriminating thought, anyone who disagrees with the Modern Liberal is *by definition* an evil discriminator.

To the Modern Liberal then, those who would argue on behalf of oil exploration when solar panels work just as well (at least as far as the people who don't do anything or make anything are concerned) are seen as not merely wrong in their choices, but evil in their hearts.

And, in fact, this is exactly the argument Barack Obama makes when he declares that anyone who questions his "green initiatives" must *want* dirtier air and water.

Similarly, to those who reside in paradise, anyone who would choose war – when everyone knows that putting a bumper sticker on your car that says "Coexist" and parking it in the faculty lot works just as well – must be some kind of racist with a sick addiction to other peoples' blood. And this is, in fact, exactly the argument made in the Leftist-penned quotation, "War is a drug..." which begins the movie *The Hurt Locker*, and in the chants of the so-called "anti-war" activists screeching "1-2-3-4, we don't want your racist war."

And since, to the infantile and naive, Islamism is just another "flavor," when Right-Thinking Americans failed to be outraged over the water boarding of an Islamic terrorist mastermind with information about the next murderous attacks, those clever folks at the

Nieman Foundation for Journalism at Harvard University could conjure no explanation other than to ask rhetorically, "Have Americans developed a *taste* for torture?" (Emphasis added.)

CHAPTER III

LEFT IN THE DUST

The chances are good that those who would eventually grow up to become Right-Thinkers finished their schooling with a similarly Leftist bent. That's just the reality of the paradise that is childhood in general, where neither toil nor intelligence is much required and the adults absorb all of the consequences of stupidity. It is even more the reality of childhood in the Modern Liberal era when even less is asked, more provided, and according to the "scientists" at the National Academy, childhood isn't over until one has, like Sandra Fluke, entered her fourth decade on the planet.

So effective is the brainwashing by the "education" system that Bloom begins his brilliant and essential book, *The Closing of the American Mind* by declaring:

> *There is one thing a professor can be absolutely certain of: almost every student entering the university believes, or says he believes, that truth is relative.*

If truth is relative, then Zinn was right – objectivity is impossible. And if objectivity is impossible, then the Modern Liberal is right: there is no reason to use one's intellect to seek out the better, for the only thing to be gained through such an effort would be just another point of view, no more valid than the last or the next.

It was only once the Right-Thinker left the paradise of childhood and entered the real world, where being right was essential to both success and survival, that the existence of the better became obvious and its pursuit and implementation imperative.

In fact, its existence quickly became so obvious that the Right-Thinker soon came to recognize that Modern Liberalism is utter nonsense, an ideology invented by people who had never done anything, taught to children who were yet to have done anything, and believed by almost no one else at any time or any place in the history of the world specifically because, in other times and in other places, people had had to do things and make things.

So ludicrous was this ideology in fact, that even some of its earliest allies, like Vladimir Lenin, couldn't help but recognize its followers to be just a bunch of "useful idiots." When even your friends call you an "idiot," it's a pretty good bet that you're an idiot.

It must not go unnoticed that what the Modern Liberal idiots were useful in accomplishing in this case was to help further empower Communism – the single most murderous ideology in all of human history.

To those who would enter the real world and go on to do things and make things, the better made itself known in the most obvious and undeniable of ways. The farmer who learned and employed the better farming techniques enjoyed a bumper crop. The farmer who didn't saw his fields lay fallow. These objective facts were not changed one whit by whatever clever rhetoric the farmer might then yet conjure. The store owner's inventory either arrived on time or it didn't – and no amount of verbal nimbleness long satisfied his customers or put food on his family's table. Put simply, the "clever" but wrong fireman soon got burned and, having been burned, learned a lesson or two. The clever but wrong academic, however, soon got tenured and, having been rewarded, sought only newer and more clever-sounding ways to repeat the same nonsense she'd believed since before she'd turned six and about which life had never once given her reason to question.

And what was true of science was equally true of God. Objective observation and reason made it simply undeniable to anyone who was allowed to think that those who were steeped in and best followed the Judeo-Christian ethos were happier, more loving, more charitable, and more successful as measured by virtually any and every metric.

This was true and obvious not only in the micro – the individual – but in the macro as well. Those nations and cultures that failed to embrace the Western-style balance between God and science suffered for it. Those, like the Soviet Union, that promoted science without God ended up in the ash heap of history, unable to survive even the remainder of the already half-over century. Nations like those of the Islamic world that were filled with "God" but devoid of science remained primitive, impoverished, and violent.

On the other hand, those nations that best embraced Western values, such as Western Europe (and now Eastern Europe, as well), Japan, South (but not North) Korea, etc., enjoyed peace, prosperity, and progress. And the two nations that had struck the best balance between God and science – America and Israel – were nearly miraculous in their accomplishments, their goodness and their greatness.

IT'S THEIR PARTY AND I'LL CRY IF I WANT TO

The people who do things and make things would soon coalesce around the newly reborn conservative movement and the party of the Republicans that housed it. The more clever Modern Liberals would become the backbone of today's Democratic Party and, while not overwhelming in numbers, they would help to transform the Democrats into a party that is always not just wrong, but as wrong as wrong can be.

The Rhetoric Industries of academia, journalism and entertainment would give the Democrats outsized power and influence and leave them in near-total control of all of the means of mass communication and indoctrination. Not the least of these was the "education" system – which the Modern Liberals would then grow into a behemoth and use to brainwash successive generations into their Cult of Indiscriminateness.

Those in the Rhetoric Industries would be joined in their coalition mostly by the lowest-income voter and the freeloaders. Though these groups are not one and the same, neither can provide much insight into how to succeed, while both are freed of the need to be right by the fact that (1) since they don't pay the taxes, they don't pay the costs of the Democrats' always-failed utopian plots and (2) since they don't run the businesses, they don't suffer the consequences of the Democrats' always-failed utopian schemes. It certainly didn't hurt that Modern Liberal policies redirected great sums of money into the pockets of these now dedicated Democratic Party voters.

That these are, in fact, the constituencies that dominate today's Democratic Party was confirmed by a piece in the *New York Times* which declared that, in his bid for reelection, Obama had "effectively jettisoned" the vast majority of the working people of America in favor of cementing:

> *A center-left coalition made up, on the one hand, of voters who have gotten ahead on the basis of educational attainment – professors, artists, designers, editors, human resources managers, lawyers, librarians, social workers, teachers and therapists, and a second, substantial constituency of lower-income voters...*

Note the use of the phrase *"educational attainment."* That is, even in the *New York Times* one finds confirmation of the fact that the fame, fortune, and, most devastatingly, the power and influence of the constituencies that form the backbone of today's Democratic Party were gained not through the crucible of real-world experience, nor was the rightness of their beliefs ever proved by the production of tangible results.

Instead, the entirety of the clever Modern Liberals' claim to their riches, power and influence comes from the fact that they'd spent the whole of their lives immersed in rhetoric, the first half being bombarded by it, the second half simply spewing it.

The professor *lectures*, the lawyer *argues*, the artist *emotes*, the therapist *consoles*, the social worker *advises*, the "community organizer" *agitates*, the editor *opines* and so on, but not a single one of the professions that comprise the most powerful and influential segment of today's Democratic Party *makes* or *mends*, *grows* or *forges, manufactures* or *cobbles*, *creates* or *produces*. Not a single one of them *does* – or ever has done – *anything*. And when you don't do anything it really is true that all you ever really need to know you learned in kindergarten.

THE POOR, RICH DEMOCRAT

The piece in *The Times* unwittingly called attention to an open secret in the Rhetoric Industries, one the clever Modern Liberals try desperately to keep hidden from the public and one that, frankly, they lie about incessantly. The "conventional wisdom" has it – mostly because it is up to those in the Rhetoric Industries to create and disseminated the "conventional wisdom" – that the Republicans are the party of "the rich" and the Democrats are the party of the working people.

In their telling, the culture war is between those despicable, bigoted, money-grubbing Republicans doing evil, non-utopian things and those oh-so-noble, salt-of-the-earth Dems who put aside their own interests for the good of the masses.

There's only one problem with the story: not only is it not true, but, like literally everything else the Modern Liberal believes (or says he believes), it is 180-degrees from the truth.

The truth is that it's the *Republicans* who are the party of the working people and it's the *Democrats* who are the party of the rich. The Democrats are also the party of the *very* rich, as well as the very, very rich and the very, very, very rich. In fact, out of the ten uber-wealthy zip codes in America – places with names like Bel Aire, Sutton Place, Nob Hill and Hyannisport – *nine* of them are in the Democrats' pocket, or, more accurately, the other way around.

What binds the working people in the middle together in the Republican Party is their shared belief in the existence of the better and the moral and practical imperative that follows to use one's intellect to seek it out and then to toil to achieve it.

What binds those at the very, very top and the very, very bottom to the Democratic Party is their shared *rejection* of the existence of the better and, in turn, their disdain for – and, in fact (as we shall see), their loathing and fear of – rational thought and physical toil.

This disdain for intellect and effort was most recently on display in Obama's famous speech in which he declared, "If you have a business, you didn't build that."

As much as the Democrats desperately tried to walk this one back, claiming it was "taken out of context," it is, in fact, an oft-repeated meme deeply rooted in Modern Liberal ideology. In fact, it had been put forth by Democratic senatorial candidate Elizabeth Warren of Massachusetts only weeks earlier and is not much different than Hillary Rodham Clinton's famous declaration that "It takes a village."

Far from being taken out of context, Obama's remarks are even more damning as one examines the further context of the speech, and his mocking attitude toward intellect and effort evident throughout:

> *I'm always struck by people who think, well, it must be because I was just so smart. There are a lot of smart people out there. It must be because I worked harder than everybody else. Let me tell you something, there are a whole bunch of hardworking people out there.*

Obama is right - there *are* a lot of smart people out there. They're the ones who create so much wealth by doing things and making things so well that so many others can live like Adam and Eve in Paradise or a child on the kindergarten playground, just being himself and doing whatever feels good. And he's right: there are "a whole bunch" of hardworking people out there – and they are almost exclusively members of the Republican Party. Again, so obvious is this fact to those in the Obama administration that they built the president's entire reelection campaign strategy around it.

THE WORK, THE WORKIN' JUST THE WORKIN' LIFE

When Adam and Eve suddenly found themselves evicted from Paradise (just as when the child finally becomes an adult), there were only two things they needed to do that they'd never needed to do before. Suddenly deprived of God's generous welfare, they had to provide for themselves by using their intellect to seek out the better things and then they had to toil to bring those better things about.

Since these are the two things that leaving Paradise required, they are the two things that the Modern Liberal is convinced are keeping him – and the world – from returning to it.

We've already discussed – and will soon return to – the Modern Liberal's antipathy toward intelligence; but still to be discussed is his disdain for toil, which is equal in every way.

Since the Right-Thinker's goal in life is to better himself and in turn the world, having a job offers him the chance to fulfill his purpose. He produces, manufactures and fixes things that fight disease and keep hunger, poverty and physical pain at bay. Having a job – and bettering himself at that job – then, is filled with great and profound rewards for the men and women of God and science.

The Modern Liberal on the other hand, not believing in the existence of the better, can see no upside to toil. To the Modern Liberal, having a job is nothing other than unmitigated hardship. In fact, here's how Bruce Springsteen - dubbed "the working man's troubadour" by the folks in the Rhetoric Industries who have the power to dub such things – describes the last Springsteen man to have ever worked for a living, his father Douglas:

> *Daddy worked his whole life*
> *for nothing but the pain...*

With "nothing but the pain" as the wages of toil, things get even worse. Since the Modern Liberal's purpose in life is to just "be himself" and to do only that which "feels good" to him at any given moment, having a job is the one and only thing that constrains him from fulfilling his life's purpose. This makes having a job not just "hard work," but nothing less than soul stealing.

Thus, despite my extensive knowledge of Springsteen's thirty-plus-year canon, I am hard-pressed to name even a single song from this supposed champion of the working man in which someone with a job isn't going through a living hell because he had to stop playing long enough to do a day's work.

In one song, "Factory," Springsteen takes us through a day in the life of a factory worker – this despite the fact that Springsteen has literally never had a job and thus doesn't know anything about the life of someone who works in a factory (or anywhere else for that matter.) Rather, the lyrics suggest what a clever and articulate man/child thinks it might *feel* like if he were ever to have to stop playing (the guitar) long enough to earn his keep.

Springsteen imagines it the way a small child might imagine it: horrific, joyless, colorless and dead, like that moment when the five-year-old's parent leans out the window and yells: "Playtime's over. Come in and do your chores."

> *Early in the morning, factory whistle blows*
> *Man rises from bed and puts on his clothes*
> *Man takes his lunch, walks out in the morning light.*
> *It's the work, the workin' it's the working life...*

Springsteen's cleverness is undeniable. His literary canniness is no doubt on display as he calls the song's protagonist "man," as in someone so stripped of his personal identity that he doesn't even have a name. And no one can question Springsteen's terrific use of imagery when, in the next stanza, he describes "man" walking through the "mansions of fear" and "mansions of pain" that Springsteen suspects people with jobs must walk through daily.

But clever words and terrific imagery don't make something true. Is Springsteen right? Is having a job really this horrific? Not according to Mike Rowe – someone who, unlike Springsteen, didn't just talk about work but actually went out and did some on his hit TV show, *Dirty Jobs*. In fact, Rowe reports that even those who do some of the most difficult and seemingly disagreeable of jobs were "Some of the happiest people

I've ever met." In other words Springsteen is – as the Modern Liberal always is – not just wrong, he's as wrong as wrong can be.

In the last stanza of "Factory," the workday mercifully comes to an end. Here Springsteen very cleverly changes his tale from the story of "man" to the story of all "men" who work for a living:

> *End of the day, [the] factory whistle cries*
> *Men walk through these gates with death in*
> *their eyes.*

Allow me another tip of the hat to Mr. Springsteen's poetic perspicacity. It is absolutely brilliant that he makes the factory whistle "cry" at this point – the cold, hard steel showing more human emotion than the lifeless zombies with no names and nothing left in them but "death" in their eyes.

So what is it exactly that Springsteen believes stripped these "men" of their identities and left them with less humanity than a piece of cold, hard steel? The singer makes no bones about it. In the final line of the song he tells us. In fact, he says it not once, not twice but six times:

> *That's the work, that's the working, that's just*
> *the working life.*
> *Yes, that's the work, that's the working, that's*
> *just the working life.*

FEAR AND LOATHING OF EARNED WAGES

Given that the reward of having a job is "nothing but the pain," and the cost is the loss of one's soul, the Modern Liberal is convinced that anyone who works for a living must fall into one of only three categories: too stupid to know, too desperate to care or too greedy to mind.

Whichever of these categories the working person falls into, then, there is clearly something "the matter" with him. In fact, this is exactly the point of the tome that the *New York Times*' theater critic, Frank Rich, called "the most prescient political book of the year."

Rich, of course, is in an unusual profession. As a theater critic he is *twice* removed from the adult world. Not only does *he* not do anything – he merely "critiques" in clever fashion what other people are doing – but the people he's critiquing don't do anything, either. Actors, like small children, spend their days *pretending* to be doing things, with no more cost to them in being wrong than there is to a five-year-old child being wrong about how tea for her tea party is made.

In fact, the very second something could even possibly go wrong, the actor is whisked off to his trailer to go and talk with his entourage and replaced by a stuntman - someone who knows how to do the things the actor is only pretending to know how to do.

The name of the book Rich found so insightful was the not-too-subtle, *What's The Matter With Kansas*. It's more than 200 pages of all sorts of *intellectualisms* by yet another member of the Rhetoric Industries about why the people of that Midwestern state don't join with the Democrats in their latest utopian schemes.

By "Kansas," of course, the author means Middle America. He means every place that's *not* Hollywood, Berkeley, Cambridge, or the Upper West Side of Manhattan. He means the regions that those in the Rhetoric Industries derisively call "fly-over country." By "Kansas," the author means those people in those places where there are farms and factories, oil wells and coal mines. What he's *really* asking is "what's the matter with the people who work?"

LOOK OUT, HE'S GONNA EXPLODE!

But the Modern Liberal doesn't just look down (literally and figuratively) on the people who toil for their reward; he fears – and ultimately loathes – them.

This is because, to the Modern Liberal, anyone who is so soulless and in so much pain as those who work for a living must be, must also be on the verge of committing horrific acts of violence. The Modern Liberal knows this because he knows that *he* would surely go insane and become violent if *he* were ever so constrained from his life's purpose by having to go to work now and then.

Springsteen's "daddy," then, not only worked his whole life for nothing but the pain, but in the next line we're told what that led to:

> *Now he walks these empty rooms*
> *Looking for something to blame.*

(Mr. Springsteen's literary skills are on display here yet again. It is truly brilliant that the song is called "Adam Raised a Cain" – Adam, being the first man to ever have had to toil who then produces Cain, the first man to have ever committed murder.)

Meanwhile, it is simply a given that "man" – the guy who works in the factory – goes home and beats his children:

> *And you just better believe, boy,*
> *Somebody's gonna get hurt tonight...*

And the garage mechanic in "The Promised Land" is on the verge of mass murder:

> *I done my best to live the right way*
> *I get up every morning, go to work each day*
> *But your eyes grow blind and your blood runs*
> *cold. Sometimes I feel so weak I just want to*
> *explode.*
> *Explode and tear this whole town apart.*
> *Take a knife and cut this pain from my heart.*
> *Find somebody itching for something to*
> *start....*

And in "Working on the Highway," the folks with jobs go out after hours either "looking to get hurt," heading into town "wearing trouble on their shirt," or, as is the case of the song's protagonist, kidnapping underage girls and raping them repeatedly.

Thus, despite the father's plea ("Son, can't you see that she's just a little girl?"), the guy with the job just can't help himself:

We lit on down to Florida and we got along
alright
One day her brothers came and got her
And they took me in a black-and-white.
The prosecutor kept the promise that he made
me on that day.
And the judge got mad and he put me straight
away.

Clearly, prosecutors who deal with all kinds of scum on a daily basis don't make particular "promises" unless the crime is truly egregious, and judges who have seen it all don't get particularly "mad" unless the act is singularly heinous.

Springsteen is too clever a poet to have chosen these words by accident. So what would make the man in the song commit such an egregious and heinous crime against a little girl? Springsteen tells us point-blank, it's because the rapist had a job – it's because he was "working on the highway."

Have you ever wondered how it could be that the Modern Liberal looks at the Tea Party movement and is convinced that its members are all about to "explode" into violence? It's not because there's the slightest bit of *objective* evidence to support their belief – in fact, the Tea Party is so peaceful that its members don't even litter.

So what is it that convinces the rich, the very rich, the very, very rich and the very, very, very rich folks in the Rhetoric Industries and those they influence that the Tea Party is constantly on the verge of violence? It is simply this: the Tea Party is a movement comprised of people who have jobs.

Conversely, have you ever wondered why, despite the body count, the multiple rapes and the assorted other violence at the Occupy Wall Street "protests" – a movement actually *named* after the Nazi occupation of Europe – the clever folks in the Rhetoric Industries believe the participants to be peaceful? It's because it's a movement comprised of folks who *don't* have jobs. The "protesters" are just "being themselves" and doing whatever "feels good" to them, and therefore their fellow Modern Liberals believe they must have the innocent souls of small children who have never been corrupted by society.

Finally, since the Modern Liberal sees anyone with a job as stupid, desperate or evil – and constantly on the verge of violence – his "support" for the working man is of the same sort as the Modern Liberal's "support" for the troops (who he's convinced can only be stupid, desperate, or bloodthirsty.) The purpose of the Modern Liberal's rhetoric and policy is nothing other than to *undermine* their missions.

The Modern Liberal attempts to undermine the mission of the troops so that they can "come home" faster – in fact, the ubiquitous bumper sticker states exactly that: "Support The Troops, Bring Them Home." Meanwhile, the Modern Liberal tries to undermine the mission of people with jobs so they can stop working, get their souls back and live in paradise by becoming

Democratic Party constituents who, like Adam and Eve and the five-year-old child, can enjoy bounty without toil.

In fact, in defending Obama's 2000-plus page health care scheme with its tens of thousands of rules, laws, regulations, mandates, dictates and diktats, Nancy Pelosi argued that one of its great features is that people could quit their jobs and go off and just be themselves and do whatever feels good to them:

> *We see it as an entrepreneurial bill, a bill that says to someone, if you want to be creative and be a musician or whatever, you can leave your work, focus on your talent, your skill, your passion, your aspirations...*

CHAPTER IV

IF YOU'RE SO SMART, WHY AIN'T YOU RICH AND, IF YOU'RE SO RICH, WHY AIN'T YOU SMART?

The clever Modern Liberal's verbal razzmatazz allows him to enjoy wealth – often great wealth – without work (or, in Springsteen's own words, "A life of leisure and a pirate's treasure"). If, however, his oratorical hocus-pocus was no longer in demand and he found himself actually having to do a real job, not only would he no longer be rich, but his infantile beliefs and lack of real world experience would see him join his ideological brethren at the very bottom of the economic strata.

This is easily proved with a simple thought exercise. Imagine if tomorrow disease, hunger, poverty and physical pain were to return. Imagine that times soon grew so tough that resources simply could no longer be so mindlessly diverted to people whose product consists of nothing more than words sometimes cleverly spoken. Imagine a time when only those who could prove their worth by producing tangible results would be rewarded.

Now ask yourself, in such a world, what would Rosie O'Donnell be doing for a living? How would Anderson Cooper be paying his bills? Is there any reason to believe – any reason whatsoever – that Al Sharpton would be doing anything other than begging for alms, or that Michael Moore wouldn't be down at the soup kitchen in a losing fight with Roseanne Barr over the last piece of bread? Can anyone even conceive of Debbie Wasserman-Schultz, Nancy Pelosi or Barney Frank being asked to return for a second day of work at a factory, a farm or anyplace else where verbal nimbleness was of no use?

Interestingly, not long ago, Springsteen did envision such a world. He sang about it on his highly *acclaimed*, cleverly *worded*, wonderfully *emoted*, but utterly ludicrous album, *Wrecking Ball*. The song was called "Jack of All Trades," and in it Springsteen describes a time in the not-so-distant future when America's economy is at the breaking point.

Throughout the tune, the singer comforts his fictional lover by telling her (I assume it's a her – does that make me sexist?) that, no matter how bad things get, they'll be able to survive because he's a "jack-of-all-trades" and thus proficient in a wide range of those skills required in such times (i.e., any other time and any other place in all of human history):

I'll hammer the nails. And I'll set the stone.
I'll harvest your crops when they're ripe and
grown.
I'll pull that engine apart and patch her up
until she's running right.
I'm a Jack of all trades. We'll be alright.

But, of course, Springsteen's *not* a jack-of-all-trades. He's a guy who sings clever little ditties about what he thinks it might *feel* like if he were a jack-of-all-trades. The truth is that Springsteen's not only not a jack-of-all-trades, he's likely not even a trey of even one of them. He doesn't do – and likely has never done – a single one of the things about which he sings. In fact, if he couldn't give his audience a little of that ol' razzle-dazzle for which he's so famous, he'd be right there at the bottom in every way with the rest of the Democratic Party constituents who share his revulsion for toil and intelligence.

Interestingly, Springsteen himself seems to be aware of this fact since every one of the skills he mentions in the song are the ones possessed by the people in the working classes who reject Modern Liberalism. Just as tellingly, Springsteen doesn't mention a single one of the "skills" required to be successful in any of the Rhetoric Industries. He must have known it would have been nothing less than laughable had he tried:

I'll opine about nails, and give an exclusive report about stones,
I'll do a one-man show about crops, when they're ripe and grown.
I'll give a lecture to the car's engine, all through the night.
I'll talk and I'll talk, dear. I'm a tenured professor, so we'll be alright.

I'M A VICTIM, YOU'RE A VICTIM, HE'S A VICTIM, SHE'S A VICTIM WOULDN'T YOU LIKE TO BE A VICTIM, TOO?

Despite having been born into a world as close to paradise as any human being since Adam and Eve, the Modern Liberal is still somehow convinced that he's history's greatest victim. In fact, according to the exhaustive research of then-Liberal statistician Arthur C. Brooks, the Democratic Party is now nothing more than a "coalition of groups that *define* themselves as victims of social and economic forces." (Emphasis added.)

It's easy to understand why those in the lower half of the economically bipolar Democratic Party are convinced that they're victims. After all, having been told that they were born morally perfect and they needn't learn anything more than they already knew by the time they'd reached the age of six, they are left to wonder why it is that everyone else in America is faring so much better than they are.

Besides, anyone who buys into the ideology that the True Believers promote – the idea that if you have a successful business you didn't build it – is going to be convinced that he's a victim because he's left only to ask, "Well, then, who *did* build it?" and then, "and why didn't they build one for *me*?"

And since he was raised to believe that there is no right or wrong, the Modern Liberal at the bottom of the economic strata knows that his failures can't be the result of anything wrong that he's *done*. Since it can't be anything he's done, then the *only* possible explanation for his failure is that it's because of who he *is*. It simply *must* be "racism" or "sexism" or "homophobia" or "xenophobia" because, to the members of the Cult of Indiscriminateness, it can be nothing else.

For example, if the Modern Liberals have it right and out-of-wedlock births are really nothing more than a different "lifestyle choice" – another "flavor" no better and no worse than any other – then the *only* explanation for the higher percentage of single mothers living at or below the "poverty" line is that there's some sort of "War on Women." Not surprisingly, then, single mothers (but not married women and even less so married women with children) constitute one of the Democratic Party's most loyal constituencies.

Similarly, if, as Gloria Steinem famously said, "A women needs a man like a fish needs a bicycle" and the nearly 80 percent out-of-wedlock birth rate in the Black community is of no consequence, then the *only* possible explanation for the higher percentage of Blacks living in "poverty" is that America is a "racist" society. Again, not surprisingly, Blacks constitute another of the Democratic Party's most loyal constituencies.

And since this is the *only* possible explanation, there is no reason for the Modern Liberal to engage his intellect to discover the true and rightful answers. In fact, as far as the Modern Liberal is concerned, the only thing that's left to be done is for the clever folks in the Rhetoric Industries to use their oratorical and literary canniness to invent a sophisticated-sounding narrative that "proves" this victimization.

It's a narrative that they'll then teach as the "truth" in the schools, report as "fact" in the news, emote with great sincerity in their concerts, movies and plays and use to make law whenever and wherever they're in power and which the Mindless Foot Soldiers will then mindlessly embrace.

THE PITIFUL PRINCE OF BEL AIRE

What is perhaps less obvious is the cause of the sense of victimization of those in the Rhetoric Industries who have been blessed with the most luxurious lives in the history of the world in exchange for doing quite literally nothing at all. If anyone in human history should feel *less* victimized by reality, it seems it should be the rich, the very rich, the very, very rich and the very, very, very rich people whose wealth has accrued wholly without toil.

So how do people who do nothing and yet live the most carefree and luxurious lifestyles in all of human history see themselves as victims? Here's how:

Since those in the Rhetoric Industries know that they don't do anything or make anything, they know that none of the world's problems can be any of *their* doing or *their* making. Therefore, to the rich, the very rich, the very, very rich and the very, very, very rich Modern Liberals in the Rhetoric Industries, *anything* that is even the *slightest* bit less than utopian in their lives or in the world must not only be the doing and making of someone else, but it must be the fault of someone with a sick taste for everything that is less than utopian.

George Clooney, for example, knows that since he doesn't do anything or make anything, none of the pollution anywhere in the world can be the least bit *his* fault. If there's even a drop of pollution sullying his pristine paradise, then, he knows that it must not only be of someone else's doing and making, but that his "victimizer" must have some sort of sick "taste" for pollution or be so greedy that he'd be willing to destroy paradise just for a few extra bucks.

Professor Henry Gates knows that, since he doesn't do anything or make anything, none of the pharmaceuticals that have unintended side effects can be any of *his* doing or *his* making. Any drug that causes even the slightest unpleasant reaction, then, must not only be someone else's fault, but that person must have some sort of sick taste for causing unpleasant side effects, or just be so evil and greedy that he doesn't care who he poisons.

Nancy Pelosi knows that since she doesn't do anything or make anything – and never once has – that if someone gets injured in a mining accident, or if a car malfunctions or a child has a bad reaction to peanut butter – if *anything* goes wrong *anywhere* in the world – it can't be any of *her* doing or making; therefore it has to be someone else's fault – someone with something "the matter" with them who might just be on the verge of violence to boot.

Everyone in the Democratic Party, then, is convinced that he or she is a victim, and every one of them agrees on who their victimizers are: the men and women of God and science who do things and make things. Their victimizers are the people who, because they live in the real word, have to engage in discriminating thought and choose the best (but by definition not utopian) answer.

The Modern Liberal at the bottom believes himself to be victimized by a society that didn't build a successful business (or life) for him, and the rich, the very rich, the very, very rich and the very, very, very rich Modern Liberals believe that they are the victims of people who are intentionally denying them the utopia to which their infantile belief system and grandiose sense of self-esteem convinces them would be theirs if only everyone else would, like them, just not do anything or make anything.

Either way, the Modern Liberal is convinced that there's something the matter with the people of God and science who do things and make things and therefore, for the sake of peace, "social justice" and their utopian dreams (as well as for the sake of the working people themselves who are too stupid or too desperate to know what's best for them), they must be stopped.

CULTURE WAR, WHAT IS IT GOOD FOR?

That the culture war is the Modern Liberal's war against the people of God and science who do things and make things – and not against, say, "income inequality," or on behalf of "the environment," as they cleverly claim – is easily proved by examining the targets that the Modern Liberals select for their very selective "outrage."

If it were truly "income inequality" that the Modern Liberals care so much about, then why isn't there an "Occupy Hollywood" movement? After all, Hollywood is a place of such great income disparity that while a handful of the "haves" live in palatial estates seemingly modeled after the *Taj Mahal*, thousands upon thousands of "have-nots" stand – often soaked and shivering – on highway exit ramps holding signs reading: "Will Work for Food."

If it were the "unjust distribution of wealth" that was really the concern of the Modern Liberals, then why is there not a peep on the college campuses where academia engorges itself on the futures of the young – leaving America's twenty-two-year-olds a quarter million dollars in debt as the schools add another billion to their coffers?

And if "income inequality" was actually the issue, why is there such outrage at the oil and pharmaceutical company executives who at least keep us warm at night and heal our sick as they take our money, but not a protester to be found questioning the career politicians who produce nothing and yet have somehow become multimillionaires just about all?

If "income disparity" were truly the issue, the Modern Liberals' choice of targets appears contradictory. But as Ayn Rand rightly noted, "there are no contradictions." "If you think you've found a contradiction," Rand advises, "you must question your supposition."

The targets of the Modern Liberals are only contradictory if one starts with the supposition that the Modern Liberal cares about income inequality. Once one recognizes that theirs is a war against the people of God and science who do things and make things – and the practices, values, and beliefs that have evolved over time from their individual and collective experiences – the contradictions all disappear. Suddenly the absence of anger (or seemingly even displeasure) with the rich, the very rich, the very, very rich and the very, very, very rich in the Rhetoric Industries makes perfect sense, as does the seeming contradiction of multimillionaire movie stars and other *one-percenters* identifying themselves with a cause that claims to be against rich people.

Similarly, if one buys into the supposition that the Modern Liberals' "environmental" policies are meant to stem things like "manmade global warming," then Al

Gore's traipsing around the globe in private jets, driving to his multimillion-dollar paydays in caravans of gas-guzzling SUVs and leaving both a personal and professional "carbon footprint" bigger than Sasquatch's should see him a person of derision among the folks on the Left. In fact, they should ride him out of town on a (high speed) rail.

Instead Gore remains a god of the "environmental" movement and the Democratic Party that houses it. How is one to explain this seeming contradiction? By rethinking one's supposition.

Once one recognizes that the "environmental" movement has nothing whatsoever to do with protecting the ecology and is just another fig leaf designed to cover the Modern Liberal's true intent, the contradictions all disappear. Since the purpose of the Modern Liberal's "environmental" policies is nothing other than to further shackle the people of God and science who do things and make things Gore's wanton disregard for the environment is of no concern to them.

CONCLUSION

In its simplest form, the culture war is a war being waged by the people who don't do or make anything against the people who do and make everything. And while this is not a wholly novel observation (Rand said it was a war waged by the "Looters" against the "Producers," while Peter Schweizer demonstrated that it's a war being waged by the "Takers" against the "Makers"), what is essential in understanding how the Modern Liberal "thinks" – and what it is about this thinking that leaves him no choice but to side at every turn with all that is evil, failed and wrong and against all that is good, right, and successful – is just a quarter-turn of the screw deeper.

The essential element is found in the relationship to the truth that one has whether they do things and makes things or whether they spend their lives just talking about the people who do things and make things.

To those who do things and make things, the truth is absolutely essential. Clever verbiage may be entertaining but it does nothing to help the farmer or the businessman, the fireman or the cop, the florist or the construction worker, the factory foreman or the electrician do his job well and do it in safety.

To those who don't do anything or make anything, however, the truth not only serves no purpose, it is, in fact, the enemy. This is why Zinn knew it to be "undesirable" and why the True Believers sought to brainwash the children into not seeking it.

To those who subscribe to the first part of Zinn's dictum – the Mindless Foot Soldiers who believe objectivity is impossible – the truth is evil because, since it is unknowable, those who seek it are fools and those who claim to have found it are bigots, phobics or greedy liars.

To those who subscribe to the second half of Zinn's dictum – the True Believer who recognizes objectivity is undesirable – the truth is evil because he's convinced it is the one and only thing standing in the way of man's return to Eden.

CHAPTER V

THE MINDLESS FOOT SOLDIER

Not long ago, the then-anchor of a major television news program began a symposium on "Islam in America" by apologizing to the Muslim panelists for the "stupidity," "bigotry," "prejudice," "hate," and "Islamophobia" she had witnessed during the then-ongoing debate over the wisdom and propriety of allowing a mosque to be built that would tower over the remains of thousands of innocents killed in the name of Islam only a short time before.

When she'd finished supplicating herself before these Muslim leaders, the highly acclaimed newswoman caught her breath and added: "And I'm embarrassed to admit it, but I don't know anything about Islam."

As hard as it may be to believe that someone managing a major news program and reading the top stories from a teleprompter every night doesn't know *anything* about the ideology at the center of virtually every terrorist attack of the past many decades and literally every war raging on the planet today, for the sake of argument, we'll take her at her word.

This, however, raises several important questions. First, given her profession and position, why didn't she feel the need to *learn* a few things about so vital an issue? Second, if she doesn't know anything about the issue, how did she come to support the building of the mosque in the first place? And finally, how is it that, knowing nothing about the matter, she was nonetheless so certain of her stance that she was convinced that anyone who disagreed with her – many of them actual experts on the subject, such as Pamela Geller, Frank Gaffney, Steven Emerson, Daniel Pipes and Robert Spencer – were not only wrong in their conclusions but bigots and phobics in their hearts?

The answer is found in the Four Laws of the Unified Field Theory and its corollaries.

THE FIRST LAW

*Indiscriminateness – the total rejection of the
intellectual process – is an absolute moral imperative.*

In *The Closing of the American Mind*, Professor Bloom was trying to explain why it was that suddenly, in the 1980s, his students were all so stupid. Bloom didn't use that word of course – he's more diplomatic than I am. What he said was that, having been involved in academia since the 1940s, he knew that what was true of the university from its inception a thousand years earlier, and had remained true all the way through the 1940s, '50s, '60s and even into the 1970s, was no longer true of the university then.

Bloom writes that, prior to the 1980s, the purpose of a child delaying his entry into the grown-up world to continue his education at the university level was to be a "scholar" – that is, he was there "to use his intellect to seek out the better." The child put off real world experience to spend time engaging his mind – to research, discuss, and think deeply – in order to discover the better art, the better literature, the better science, the better forms of governance, the better theologies, the better ideologies, the better ways of finance, and so on.

Suddenly in the 1980's – by no coincidence the very moment when the first Children of the Sixties were first reaching their positions of greatest power and influence and the first children of the Children of the Sixties were first beginning to matriculate – not only was the purpose of attending the university no longer to use one's intellect to seek out the better, but now virtually every university student vehemently, virulently, and sometimes even violently denied the very existence of the better. Bloom concluded that this was because they had been raised to believe that "indiscriminateness is a moral imperative because its opposite is discrimination."

In the 1980s, discriminating thought was, for all intents and purposes, outlawed. It had long been on the outs in certain oddball circles: most recently the Beatniks and the Hippies had formed small pockets of gallivanting idiots; but the idea had been around at least since Rousseau in the 1700s. But an ideology of intentional and abject stupidity found little traction in a world filled with all sorts of real-world perils that everyone knew could only be avoided through the study of the immutable laws of God and science and the practice of what was then rightly learned.

But with the miraculous advances of the previous few decades (and the particular accomplishments of the men and women of God and science who were rightly recognized as the "Greatest Generation" of all) having all but vanquished the dire consequences of disease, hunger, poverty, and physical pain, an ideology that sought to re-create Paradise by eliminating rational thought finally was able to find fertile ground.

The rationale used to outlaw reason was that anything a person thinks is going to have been so tainted by his personal prejudices – prejudices borne of such things as the color of his skin, the nation of his ancestry, his economic status, his height, weight, sex and so on – that the only way for him not to be an evil bigot was for him to never think at all. This is what Zinn meant when he proclaimed objectivity "impossible," and what Rand spoofed in *Atlas Shrugged* by having one of the more pompous pseudo-intellectuals title his book "Why Do You Think You Think?" and offer up bon mots like "Reason is an irrational idea."

Those who sold this rationale were the True Believers. Those who bought into it became their Mindless Foot Soldiers.

YEAH, BUT IS OBJECTIVITY OBJECTIVELY UNDESIRABLE?

The True Believer is also convinced that indiscriminateness is a moral imperative, but it's for a very different reason. The True Believer looks back on the thousands and thousands of years of human history and, while he often knows very little about it (and cares even less), there is one thing about which he is absolutely certain: none of the ideas – none of the religions, philosophies, ideologies, forms of governance, or anything else – that mankind has ever conceived has succeeded in creating a world devoid of war, poverty, crime, and injustice.

This has left the True Believer convinced that, since every idea man has ever thought of has "proved" to be wrong, the real cause of war, poverty, crime, and injustice must be found – in fact can only be found – in the attempt to be right.

If no one ever thought he was right, the True Believer is convinced, there'd be nothing for people to disagree about. If people didn't disagree, then surely they wouldn't fight, and if they didn't fight, then of course they'd never go to war.

It only follows then (or so the True Believer is positive) that, without war, there'd be no poverty; without poverty, there'd be no crime; without crime there'd be no injustice, and so on. His, then, is a Utopian Vision. And all that's required to usher in this utopia is the elimination of all of the tools of the intellect – God and science, art and craft, truth and beauty, etc. – that Right-Thinking people use in their quest to better themselves, and in turn, to better the world.

Here's how Bloom describes the True Believer's utopian vision:

> *All the world was mad in the past. Men always thought they were right and that led to wars, persecution, slavery, xenophobia, racism and chauvinism. The point [today] is not to correct the mistakes and actually be right, rather it is not to think that you are right at all...*

Rabbi Joshua Hammerman articulated the True Believer's concerns well:

> *Emboldened faithful can do insane things, like burning mosques, bashing gays and indiscriminately banishing immigrants."*

To prevent such horrors (and others like them), then, the Modern Liberal can either eliminate the things that people have faith in or eliminate the evidence that emboldens them in their faith. As we shall discuss forthwith, the Modern Liberal would prefer the former, but realities are such that he must focus on the latter.

It is instructive to note, by the way, just what it was that saw Hammerman rush to put pen to paper to warn the world about the terrible threat of the "emboldened faithful" at that particular moment. It wasn't a gathering of the Ku Klux Klan, nor was it a meeting of the Neo-Nazis. It was, in fact, the Rabbi's terror over the possibility that the Denver Broncos might win a football game. I kid you not:

> *If (Tim) Tebow wins the Super Bowl, against all odds, it will buoy his faithful, and emboldened faithful can do insane things, like burning mosques, bashing gays and indiscriminately banishing immigrants...*

What must not be missed is that Hammerman's argument is no different from the one that Spencer, Pipes, Gaffney, Emerson and Geller (et al.) made that the prominent newswoman not only mindlessly pooh-poohed, but inevitably decried as bigotry and phobia.

The scholars were concerned that a "victory mosque" towering over the remains of the thousands and thousands of infidels massacred in the name of Islam might embolden other Islamists to press their declared and required jihad against those they deem to be the Great Satan.

Hammerman, on the other hand, was worried that America's Christians might set off on an unprecedented series of violent, racist, homophobic and Islamophobic rampages in utter opposition to the teaching of their faith if their favorite quarterback happened to lead his team to victory in a ball game.

How did these two Modern Liberals – the successful newswoman and the Rabbi – come to their conclusions? How did someone who knows nothing about the issue come to champion the most violent ideology on the planet and the Rabbi come to have such terrible fears about the people who created so welcoming a land that immigrants from around the world flock here to escape persecution and enjoy liberty?

The full answer to that question comes in just a few more pages. For now, I think we can agree: neither conclusion was the product of intellect. In fact, they seem to be (and in fact are) the product of nothing other than the inevitable anti-good/pro-evil bigotry and phobia guaranteed by the laws of the Unified Field Theory of Liberalism. These Modern Liberals see their mindless bigotries and phobias as not only "right" but the epitome of morality because they were produced without the slightest bit of intelligence.

It all seems like insanity (in fact, William Buckley called it "The Mania"). It's Alice in Wonderland stuff. It's as if, in Prager's words, "The world is upside down." But it's not. Modern Liberalism is upside down, and, at least in the case of the True Believer, it is intentionally so. And, unfortunately, since the end of World War II, the Modern Liberal has gained more and more control of the once free world.

THE BLUEPRINT FOR UTOPIA

The True Believer's Blueprint for Utopia was perfectly articulated in one of the most popular and beloved anthems of the Modern Liberal era – John Lennon's "Imagine."

In "Imagine," Lennon promises the world paradise, but only once people are left with nothing to believe in or care about.

Thus, according to Lennon's plan, mankind can return to Eden, but only after all consideration of the better forms of governance is ended. That's what having "no countries" would accomplish.

Notice that Lennon does not discriminate between right and wrong, better and worse or good and evil. It's not what countries *do* that matters; it's countries themselves, so that there is no difference to Lennon between America – which has provided the world with the food, medicines and technological advances that has virtually ended all disease, hunger, poverty and pain – and Nazi Germany which gave the world nothing but misery and death.

And, according to Lennon, Paradise would be regained, but only if all discussion of the better moral codes ceased. That's what having "no religion" would do. Again, note that there is no moral or intellectual distinction drawn between a religion that teaches

"Love thy neighbor" and has brought us Western Civilization and one that preaches "Kill all infidels" and has brought us every war on the planet today.

Essential to the True Believer's Blueprint for Utopia – and a central part of every Leftist ideology from before Lenin to after Lennon – is having "no possessions." This is because possessions serve as tangible evidence of having engaged in the better (more productive) behaviors. Since the Modern Liberal's paradise requires denying the existence of the better, all behaviors – hard work and sloth, ingenuity and chicanery, sobriety and drug addiction – must be equally and indiscriminately rewarded.

To usher in Utopia, the True Believer knows that he must squelch all inquiry into the past, for history provides ample evidence of the existence of the better. He must also sever all ties to the future, for the Modern Liberal knows that caring for the well-being of one's children leads to seeking out and championing the better, if not for oneself than for one's progeny. This is why the Modern Liberal knows, and Lennon declares, that heaven on Earth requires "all the people living for today."

In the Modern Liberal paradise that Lennon describes to perfection, there is no reason to try to better oneself because there is no such thing as the better. You can, in fact, spend your life just "being yourself" and doing whatever "feels good" at any given moment, for no matter what you do, you will be equally rewarded. It's all very much like the Garden of Eden. It's exactly like the kindergarten classroom.

Lennon sums up the True Believer's Blueprint for Utopia perfectly in one of the final lines from the song when he promises a return to Paradise, but only once anything and everything that mankind values has been so devalued that there's "nothing to kill or die for."

THE EMBOLDENED AND THE BEAUTIFUL

The True Believer knows, of course, that not all countries are going to disappear overnight just because he imagines it. And he knows that not all religions are going to be vanquished in an instant just because of the power of his mind. He knows that, for all his clever bumper sticker sloganeering, if he's going to succeed in ushering in the utopia he dreams of, he's going to have to do more than just "visualize world peace;" he's going to have to take action.

Unable to quickly or easily achieve their preferred goal – the elimination of all beliefs – the True Believers turned to "Plan B": the elimination of the evidence that emboldens people in their convictions.

This they would accomplish by working only and always for one purpose: to use their powers in the Rhetoric Industries and beyond to elevate the lesser in esteem, stature, power, and reward, while, at the same time, denigrating and weakening all that is good, right, successful.

By doing so, the True Believer intends to make all things appear to "meet in the middle," with nothing seen as better or worse than anything else, and surely nothing as so good and right as to be worthy of fighting to defend, nor anything so evil and wrong that it becomes necessary to go to war to prevent its spread. By doing so, peace will reign and, with it, the end of all poverty, crime and injustice.

You will recognize this as both the paradigm and the purpose of perhaps the most successful Modern Liberal motion picture of all time. There is no one – literally no one – who believes that Michael Moore's *Fahrenheit 9-11* was an honest attempt to accurately portray the real people and the real events of that horrific day and its aftermath.

Everyone knows that Moore is a Modern Liberal who used his ample skills as a filmmaker to cherry-pick the facts, manipulate the evidence and offer an agenda-driven line of narrative. And what was that agenda? It was to make America look less good than she, in fact, is while concurrently making Saddam appear less evil than he, in fact, was. The purpose was to make them both appear to "meet in the middle," leaving the United States seeming not so good as to be worth fighting for, and Saddam not so evil as to require warring against and thus "keeping the peace."

That this pro-evil, anti-good agenda is not just held by one perverse man, but is endemic to the Modern Liberal movement and the Democratic Party it controls is easily proved.

In *Up From Liberalism*, William Buckley (in his famously understated way) offered a formula for determining if a practice or a policy is anything more than a reflection of certain individuals within a movement or a reflection of the movement as a whole:

If... [an individual's] publicly known irresponsibilities do not serve to blemish that individual's reputation amongst his co-ideologists, then it is fair to assume that his practice is an acceptable practice of the movement.

When, for example, Scott Roeder gunned down the late-term abortionist George Tiller, as much as the Liberals attempted to pin his atrocity on the Christian community and the Christian value system as a whole, the response from his fellow Christians – sadness, outrage, and condemnation – made clear that, while they may have shared Roeder's disdain for late-term abortions, his *actions* were beyond the pale and in no way a reflection of Christians or the Christian movement itself.

Far from Moore's well-known pro-evil/anti-good lies "blemishing" his reputation among his co-ideologists, however, they are exactly what made him a superstar in the Modern Liberal movement.

The fact that, rather than Moore being shunned for his pro-Saddam/anti-American propaganda, the Democratic Party leadership gave him a standing ovation, his ideological brethren lavished him with near-unanimous rave reviews in the media, and Modern Liberal icon Jimmy Carter offered him a seat of "honor" at the Democratic Party's national convention makes clear that lying on behalf of evil and against the good is endemic to the Democratic Party and the Modern Liberal movement that controls it.

Not to be missed is the fact that Moore's movie would have been exactly the same whether he was a True Believer or a Mindless Foot Soldier. The only difference would have been found in his motive. If Moore is a True Believer, he would have seen his pro-evil/anti-good lies to be in the service of the Modern Liberal's Blueprint for Utopia. If he's just another Mindless Foot Soldier he would have had to start and end his "thinking" with the belief that America and Saddam's Iraq are equally right, and then he'd have cherry-picked the facts and manipulated the evidence to tell that "true" story.

THE SECOND LAW

The more clever of the losers may then offer "brilliant" theories about how the con was pulled but the purpose of their thinking isn't to determine if a wrong was committed, only to invent the most adult-sounding explanation for how the rip-off worked.

Still, it's a long way from the fact that the Modern Liberal eschews rational thought to the fact that he sides at every turn with all that is evil, failed and wrong and against all that is good, right and successful. Why doesn't his lack of true intellectual engagement and real-world experience or his Blueprint for Utopia lead him to more random policies? Why don't his infantile beliefs and utopian ideology see him fall sometimes on the side of right, sometimes on the side of wrong and sometimes just somewhere in the middle?

The reason is both simple and irrefutable: if nothing – no person, no culture, no religion, no form of governance, no work of art, no familial construct, etc. – is better or worse than any other, then the Modern Liberal has no explanation for real-world success and failure.

To those who deny the existence of the better, the simple fact that something has succeeded is all the proof that's required for them to conclude that some injustice must have taken place. After all, why should a person, business, culture, religion or nation succeed if it's not better than any other?

For the same reason, to those who do not engage in discriminating thought, failure is proved to be an injustice by nothing other than the fact that it has failed. Again, why should something fail if it's not worse than anything else?

And it only follows, then, that if success and failure are the result of injustice, then *great* success and *great* failure can be nothing other than the result of *great* injustice. And, at a certain point, great and *sustained* success and failure proves to the Modern Liberal not only that great and sustained injustices have taken place, but that that these injustices (whatever they were) were intentional and part of some evil conspiracy.

Why an evil conspiracy? Think about it this way: Let's say you're playing roulette. Your expectation is that no number is better than another and that each and every number should have an equally good chance of winning on any and every spin. When on the first spin one person wins and another person loses, it's not "fair," but neither is it a big deal. One thing is for sure, though – it can't be said that the winner won because he's smarter or better or harder working than is the loser.

But what if that same number was to come up ten times in a row and the same people won and lost on each of those spins? While this might not yet prove conspiracy, it's most certainly a "cosmic" injustice. Looking over at the winners' stacks, the losers might utter the Obamaism: "You didn't build that," and like Obama and his supporters, militate for "sharing the wealth."

But what if this goes on and on and the same number comes up *fifty* times in a row with all the same people winning and losing? This simply *can't* just be luck. The game has simply *got* to be fixed, and the winners simply *must* have been in on it. Now, not only is the call for "income redistribution" loud and insistent, but so, too, is the call for retribution against the conspirators. Soon they might even decide to "Occupy Las Vegas."

LIBERAL JUSTICE IS BLIND...AND VERY DUMB

Of course, life isn't roulette and there *are* better and worse beliefs and practices but the Mindless Foot Soldier cannot allow himself to see it, while the True Believer may see it but cannot allow himself to admit it (at least not publicly.)

It is a "moral imperative," then, to both groups of Modern Liberals that they blindly support *any* policy that is designed to deny the successful the "ill-gotten" fruits of their success, with the greater success the target of greater attacks and the *most* successful the target of not only the *most* withering and sustained assaults and mindless enmity, but demands for retribution as well.

And the same is true in the inverse. The Modern Liberal has no choice but to blindly support *any* policy meant to reward and compensate the failures for the injustices that simply must have befallen them, with the greater failures receiving more sympathy and compensation and the greatest of all failures deserving not only the greatest reward but the right to avenge their victimizers.

So great is this "moral imperative" in fact, that punishing the successful and rewarding the failed is not only a priority it is the Modern Liberal's *top* priority - with no other consideration even coming in second.

This is why, for example, when President Obama was asked if it could be proved to his satisfaction that lowering the capital gains tax rate would - as all reason and objective evidence suggests - increase government revenue, would he then support doing so? Obama said he wouldn't. Obama explained, "It's a matter of fairness."

To the Modern Liberal - the True Believer and the Mindless alike - remedying the "injustice" that is success and failure is so much an imperative that the President of the United States would prefer its accomplishment to paring down the national debt, cutting the deficit, repairing the nation's infrastructure or supplying more money to the public schools.

EVIL, WOE-MAN

What is true of success and failure is equally true (and even more imperative) of good and evil. Since to the indiscriminate, good and evil are (or at least must be said to be) nothing more than matters of personal taste, *anything* that society recognizes as good can only be thought so because of society's bigotries, while *anything* society recognizes as evil can only be the victim of society's phobias.

It is out of a sense of justice then, that the Modern Liberal sees his job as nothing more than to denigrate everything society recognizes as good for no other reason than that society recognizes it to be good. At the same time he must work to elevate in esteem and stature, power and reward, everything that society recognizes as evil for no other reason than that society recognizes it to be evil. Sowell had it right again when he described the "thought process" behind Modern Liberal policies:

> *That which is held in esteem qualifies to be their target; that which is held in disdain qualifies to be their mascot.*

To paraphrase the philosopher Dinesh D'Souza, "The indiscriminate must become de facto apologists for tyranny." For exactly the same reason, the indiscriminate must at the same time become de facto antagonists to liberty. In fact, the indiscriminate must

109

become de facto apologists for *everything* that is evil, failed, or wrong while concurrently acting as de facto antagonists to *everything* that is good, right, or successful.

CHAPTER VI

THE THIRD LAW

All Modern Liberal policies occur in tandem, with every effort meant to reward the lesser met with an equal and opposite campaign against the better.

To understand how this works, let's consider the women of the daytime chat show, *The View* (a program predicated entirely on the Modern Liberal notion that one need know absolutely nothing about anything in order to be deemed an expert on anything and everything).

One day, when he was a guest on the program, Bill O'Reilly committed the cardinal sin of Modern Liberalism: he spoke the objective truth. He said that it was the Muslims who attacked America on 9-11. I'm glad he did, because up until then, I'd thought it might have been the Amish.

The speaking of this simple fact was seen as so outrageous by the bitter women with the stunningly ironic names of "Joy" and "Whoopi" that they marched off the stage in high dudgeon. As my friend Seth Swirsky would say, "They took their ball and went home."

Finally, after a few minutes of coaxing, Barbara Walters (whose *fifty years* of having never done anything makes her the *dean* of the program) was able to coax the women back onto the set. But they were still outraged and all aflutter as they tried desperately to counter the simple truth with clever rhetoric.

The ladies' first gambit was to offer the oft-heard Liberal argument that it wasn't Muslims who attacked America on 9-11 because, well, "Did *every* Muslim attack us?" Of course not. That would be ridiculous. America doesn't have that many planes.

But the idea that for something to be true it must be true of everything in that category would mean that cigarettes don't cause cancer since not everyone who smokes a cigarette gets cancer, drunk driving doesn't cause car accidents because not every drunk driver has an accident, and that gunshots to the head from close range don't cause death because not *everyone* who is shot in the head at close range dies.

Obviously, there's *something* about these things that so increases the chances of a bad outcome that it is undeniable that they are the cause. And just as obviously there is *something* about Islam that so dramatically increases a person's chances of ending up with their head in a basket, one or more of their hands in the trash bin, their clitoris in a dumpster, a slit in their throats, thousands of innocents massacred on their street, or a couple of airplanes in their conference room, that to deny that Islam causes violence is about as silly as arguing that being shot in the head doesn't cause death.

Nonetheless they tried and, for obvious reasons, O'Reilly was able to easily bat that argument away. So the women changed tack. Since they had tried and failed to cover up Islam's role in the massacres of 9-11, they had only one other option: they had to try and prove America's religion, Christianity, creates terrorists, too. If they could prove that, then Islam would no more be the cause of terror than any other faith and 9-11 could be rightly called just another "man-caused," not Muslim-caused "disaster."

The problem for Goldberg and Behar however, was that since Christianity *doesn't* cause terrorism, the best they could do by way of evidence was to dredge up a guy – from all the way back a couple of decades ago – who wasn't Christian but who did happen to have a Christian-sounding name: Timothy McVeigh.

The entire farce played out exactly as the Unified Field Theory anticipated. 1) The women wouldn't use their intellect to discriminate between religions because that would be "discrimination." 2) Since they couldn't discriminate, when O'Reilly spoke the truth they simply had to take the opposite side. This required them to 3) not only side with the ideology responsible for virtually every atrocity committed anywhere on the planet today, but to concurrently attack a true religion of peace, Christianity. And, finally, 4) as the Fourth Law requires (as discussed in the next chapter), in order to defend the terrorists, the ladies had to ascribe to the good Christians the exact crime that they, as Modern Liberals, had no choice but to be mindlessly defending when committed by the Muslims.

That Behar and Goldberg didn't care about truth, justice, morality, decency, or anything other than to exonerate Islam and indict Christianity at all costs is proved by the seemingly contradictory standard of evidence they employed in their arguments.

While virtually every terrorist attack of their lifetimes, every war on the planet today, the horrors playing out in Libya, Syria, the Sudan and Iran, and the horrific violence in literally every other Islamic nation on earth was not considered by them enough proof to conclude that Islam causes terrorism, a single guy from a previous century with a Christian-sounding name was more than enough proof for them to argue that Christianity does. And to hate – nothing less than hate – anyone (in this case O'Reilly) who disagreed.

Are Behar and Goldberg part of some evil conspiracy to bring down America? Are they "Marxists" trying to bring Communism to the world? No, they're idiots in a profession where intelligence was simply not a requisite for their success. They are Mindless Foot Soldiers for a Cult of Indiscriminateness that requires them to side with evil, failure and wrong and against the good, right and successful.

THE FOURTH LAW

The Modern Liberal will ascribe to the better the negative qualities associated with the lesser, while concurrently ascribing to the lesser the positive qualities found in the better.

As we have just seen, because the Modern Liberal feels he must protect the evil, failed, and wrong, he simply has no choice but to do so by attacking the good, right, and successful. But it's not enough for the Modern Liberal to simply ascribe just a certain measure of guilt to the good and innocent; he must elevate the wrongs he ascribes to the innocent to exactly the level of the wrong he is, as a Modern Liberal, invariably defending.

That is, in order for Goldberg and Behar to succeed in exonerating Islam of its role in creating terrorists, they couldn't have just argued that Christians do some bad things sometimes, too. In order to defend the Islamic terrorists they could do nothing less than attempt to prove that Christians are terrorists, too.

To understand how this Fourth Law of the Unified Field Theory of Liberalism works, it is helpful to think about the requirements for claiming "justifiable homicide" in America's courts.

If I intentionally shoot my neighbor, that's the heinous offense of homicide. I would likely go to jail, and perhaps for the rest of my life. Unless, of course, I can prove that the killing was justified.

In order to do this, I need to prove that I shot my neighbor because I was provoked, in which case I might be exonerated. But that would only be true if the provocation rose to the level of my act. If the provocation was merely that my neighbor was playing his music too loud, it is no defense at all.

In order for my shooting my neighbor to be considered justifiable homicide, the provocation would have to rise to the level of violence that I used to stop it.

This is why Jimmy Carter calls Israel an "apartheid" state when literally nothing could be further from the truth. Carter, knows, of course, that Israel isn't an apartheid nation, but he needs something evil to pin on the Jews to explain the evils committed by the Palestinians. If he can't justify their blowing up of civilians on buses and the mass murder of school children in their kindergarten classrooms then Carter would have to admit that there's something wrong – even evil – about the Palestinian culture. Since he's not allowed to do that, the *only* thing he can do is invent heinous wrongs supposedly committed by the Jews that "provoked" the Palestinians.

This is also the explanation for the otherwise insane attacks by Liberal college professor Ward Churchill against the victims of 9-11, who he said all deserved to be burned alive in their places of employment because every American is a "Little Eichmann."

Was Sophia Addo really a miniature version of the architect of the Holocaust? Here's how the *New York Times* described her:

> *Sophia B. Addo [came] to the United States from Ghana in 1996: a teacher of school-children in Africa, she decided to take a chance and come to New York to further her own education...She had her working papers, and landed a succession of housekeeping jobs while she improved her English. Already having passed an oral exam, she was due to take a written test on Sept. 12 to see if she was entitled to a G.E.D. certificate and college eligibility...*

Was Donna Bernaerts-Kearns really a Nazi? Nope, just a computer programmer from Hoboken, New Jersey. How about Anthony Alvarado? Nope. Here's his story according to *The Times*:

> *Anthony Alvarado lived for his son. He suffered a stroke when his son was a newborn, and was paralyzed on his right side and lost his memory. It was as if he were a child again, said his mother, Sonia Irizarry...Ms. Irizarry nursed her son back to health. "Little by little, he came back," she said.*

In fact, according to my research, not a single one of the thousands and thousands of people murdered by the Muslims on that day had any affiliation with the Nazi Party or in any way supported National Socialism.

So why did Churchill do it? Why did this very clever and wonderfully articulate member of one of the Rhetoric Industries – the very chairman of the "Ethnic Studies Department" at a major American University – engage in such vicious and obvious slander against thousands of newly massacred innocents?

It's because he simply had no choice. As a member of the Cult of Indiscriminateness he had to start and end his "thinking" with the belief (or stated belief) that Islam and Judeo-Christianity are equally right and equally valid – just two different "flavors." When the Islamists attacked, he simply had no choice but to "conclude" (or *say* he'd concluded) that the terrorists were provoked. Any other conclusion would serve as evidence that there is something wrong with Islam, which is a conclusion the Mindless Foot Soldier is not allowed to draw and the True Believer is not allowed to say for fear that it might lead to war.

But, since the multiple massacres of 9/11 were singularly heinous, Churchill needed a singularly heinous evil to pin on the innocent victims. Anything less than a miniature version of the Holocaust would not have justified the Islamists' attacks, thus every American is a "little Eichmann" not because fact or reason leads to that conclusion, but because the members of the Cult of Indiscriminateness *need* it to be true. The Mindless will believe it because they're not allowed to believe anything else, while the True Believer will sell it because their Blueprint for Utopia demands it.

CONCLUSION

In the full version of this book I go into further detail about the retardation of the Modern Liberal and how it leads him and, in fact, can only lead him, to side with all that is evil, failed and wrong and against all that is right.

I also detail the social and psychological consequences of his retardation, which manifests itself in a variety of ailments including the mental illness of adult or permanent Narcissism. In the forthcoming book, I also delve into the "Language of Indiscriminateness" which includes "political correctness" as well as the tactics Modern Liberals use and why demagoguery and intimidation are the only tools available to them as a means of persuasion. Please look for that book in the late winter/early spring of 2013.

For the first part of the Modern Liberal era, the abject stupidity of the permanently infantilized could be absorbed by a society still infused with the values of the last of the Great Generations. So long as there were a sufficient number of people of God and science doing things and making things, the Modern Liberals could remain forever like Adam and Eve in Eden or the child on the kindergarten playground. So long as there were people of God and science who could provide for them when they couldn't provide for themselves, in a world without disease, hunger, poverty or physical pain, they were sure to be safe and comfortable just being themselves and doing whatever feels good.

But with the influence of the last of the Great Generations waning with their passing years – and, more and more now, their passing from this earth – the balance has shifted. We now have successive generations of Americans who not only see intellect and toil as the cause of the world's evils, but who have never known a generation that didn't.

Today we are at a tipping point where the people of God and science will soon be overwhelmed by the demands of taking care of the permanently infantilized. It is unsustainable. If the system collapses under the weight, the future is not merely a slightly less wonderful existence, it is a return to what life had been like for the overwhelming majority of people in all other times and all other places – and still is for those in lands where the balance between God and science does not well exist. That life was described by Thomas Hobbes as "nasty, brutish and short."

We're not there yet, but we're close.

ABOUT THE AUTHOR

Evan has written and/or produced in just about every medium that exists including television, movies and documentaries. He segued into politics after 9-11 and quickly became the go-to guy for both political satire and his more serious insights into the mind of the Left, speaking at venues including the Heritage Foundation, CPAC and David Horowitz's Restoration Weekend. Evan lives in Los Angeles.

CPSIA information can be obtained at www.ICGtesting.com
Printed in the USA
LVOW011726030413

327457LV00019B/944/P

9 781480 010420